52 Activities for Exploring Values Differences

Permissions

Grateful acknowledgment is made to the authors and publishers who granted permission to include adapted versions of their activities or to use research materials to devise new activities.

Milton J. Bennett and Janet M. Bennett, Intercultural Communication Institute, Portland, Oregon

Pierre Casse, *Training for the Cross-Cultural Mind: A Handout for Cross-Cultural Trainers and Consultants*.

Executive Diversity Services, Seattle, Washington, for numerous activities and/or handouts.

Lee Gardenswartz and Anita Rowe, *Diverse Teams at Work: Capitalizing on the Power of Diversity*.

Brian P. Hall, *Personal Workbook: Understanding and Working with Values*.

Brian P. Hall and Martin L. W. Hall, *Understanding and Working with Values*.

Intercultural Press for permission to use material from the following:
  Paula Chu, in *Experiential Activities for Intercultural Learning*
  Donna Goldstein, in *Experiential Activities for Intercultural Learning*
  Daniel J. Hess, *The Whole World Guide to Culture Learning*.
  Robert L. Kohls and John Knight, *Developing Intercultural Awareness: A Cross-Cultural Training Handbook*, 2d edition.
  Paul Pedersen, in *Intercultural Sourcebook: Cross-Cultural Training Methods*, Vol. 2.
  Kurt W. Russo, ed. Florence Kluckhohn's "Value Orientations Survey" in *Finding the Middle Ground: Insights and Applications of the Value Orientations Method*.
  Craig Storti, *Figuring Foreigners Out: A Practical Guide*.

Carol Wolf, in *Experiential Activities for Intercultural Learning*.

Terrell Jones, The Pennsylvania State University.

Andre Laurent, "Reinventing Management at the Cross-Roads of Culture," The Summer Institute for Intercultural Communication.

Anita Rowe, "Understanding Diversity Blind Spots in the Performance Review."

Kristine Sullivan, presentation on Dr. Bernard Haldane's Dependable Strengths Process, Seattle University, Seattle, Washington.

Sivasailam Thiagarajan, activities presented at The Summer Institute for Intercultural Communication.

Harry C. Triandis, from research for Culture and Social Behavior.

Van Hutton, from a presentation on values presented at Seattle University, 1998.

Jaime Wurzel, 1993.

Ron Zemke, Claire Raines, and Bob Filipczak, *Generations at Work: Managing the Clash of Veterans, Boomers, Xers, and Nexters*. Performance Research Associates, Inc., AMACOM, a division of the American Management Association.

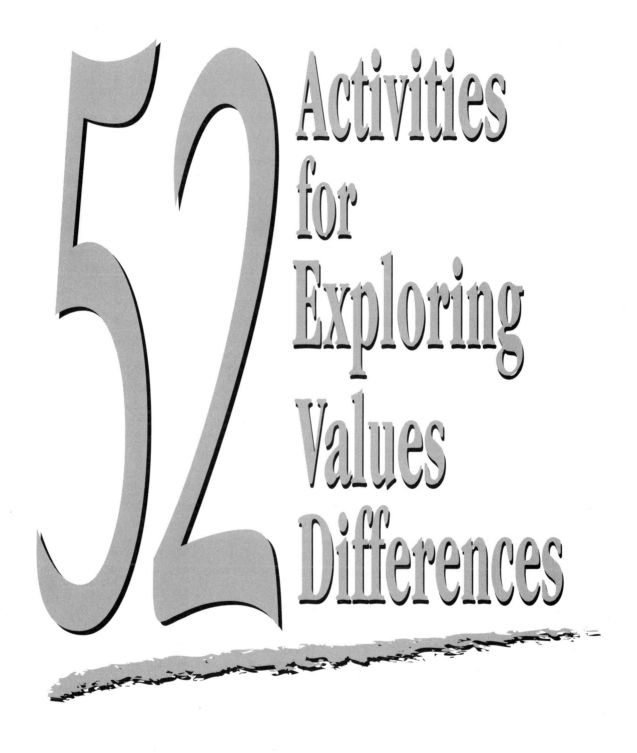

52 Activities for Exploring Values Differences

Donna M. Stringer and Patricia A. Cassiday

First published by Intercultural Press. For information contact:

Intercultural Press, Inc.
PO Box 700
Yarmouth, Maine 04096 USA
Tel: 207-846-5168
Fax: 207-846-5181
www.interculturalpress.com

Nicholas Brealey Publishing
3–5 Spafield Street
London, EC1R 4QB, UK
Tel: +44-207-239-0360
Tel: +44-207-239-0370
www.nbrealey-books.com

©2003 by Donna M. Stringer and Patricia A. Cassiday

Production and design by Patty J. Topel

Printed in the United States of America

07   06   05   04   03   1   2   3   4   5

Library of Congress Cataloging-in-Publication Data

Stringer, Donna M.
    52 activities for exploring values differences/Donna M. Stringer and Patricia A. Cassiday.
        p.   cm.
    Includes bibliographical references.
    1-877864-96-X
        1. Cross-cultural orientation—Activity programs. 2. Ethnopsychology—Study and teaching—Activity programs I. Title: Fifty-two activities for exploring values differences. II.Cassiday, Patricia A. III. Title.
    GN345.65.S77 2003
    303.48′2—dc21   2003047852

Table of Contents

Acknowledgments

This book would not have been possible without the foundation work on values by many of our colleagues and predecessors, for which we are enormously grateful. We particularly want to acknowledge the principals of Executive Diversity Services, Inc. in Seattle, Washington (Andy Reynolds, Elmer Dixon, and Linda Taylor), who have developed many of these activities over the past two decades. Faculty at The Summer Institute for Intercultural Communication in Portland, Oregon, have contributed substantially to our thinking and skills as trainers and educators, and the rich resources of books offered by Intercultural Press have been our foundation. We also thank the editorial and production team at Intercultural Press for their expertise and careful editing. We owe our enthusiasm for, and confidence in, an experiential learning approach to Sivasailam Thiagarajan, "Thiagi," to whom we are grateful. Thiagi is a master of the experiential approach, and he always encourages his students to find their own answers to the question.

We hope this book is useful to you. Please modify the activities to meet the needs of your audience—as we have through the years.

The authors have made every effort to cite and acknowledge all those from whom research, lecture material, or activities have been adapted.

Classification of Activities

	Name	Context	Time in Minutes	Risk	Purposes
1	Cultural Values	general	35	L	D, M
2	A "Jolt" of Reality	general	8–15	L	P, T, O, D, M
3	Let's Draw a House	general	20	L	P, T
4	Time Values	work	60–75	L	T, O, D
5	Age Case Study	work	60	L	P, D
6	A Value to D.I.E. For	work	60	L	P, T, D, M
7	Role Models	general	55–70	L	P, D, M
8	Saying It Makes It So	general	60–75	L	P, D, M
9	Organizations in Cultural Perspective	work	60	L	P, T, O, M
10	Cross-Cultural Values	general	60	L	P, T, D, M
11	Contrasting Values	adaptable	70–85	L	M
12	Origins of Cultural Contrasts	general	45	L	P, D, M
13	Values of Performance Feedback	work	30	L	P
14	What Do Others See?	general	60	L–M	P, D, M
15	Five Values	work	60–75	L–M	P, T, O, D, M
16	What Would You Say?	work	60	L–M	P, T
17	Generational Values	work	75–90	L–M	P, T, D
18	Team Values Assessment	work	60	L–M	P, T, D
19	International Cultural Values	work	75–120	L–M	P, D, M
20	Work Values	work	60	L–M	P, T, D, M
21	In My Family	work	60	L–M	P, T, D, M
22	Group Commandments	adaptable	60	L–M	P, T, O, D, M
23	I Am	adaptable	60	L–M	P, T, O
24	U.S. American Values	general	60	L–M	P, D
25	Performance Evaluations: How Do You Feel? What Do You Think?	work	60	L–M	P, O, D, M
26	What Is the Message?	general	35	M	P, D, M
27	Visible and Invisible Values	general	60	M	P, T, D, M

28	Similarities and Differences	general	35–40	M	P, T, D, M
29	If This Is a Value, What Will You See?	work	75	M	O, T
30	Values in Action	work	90	M	T, O, D
31	Sorting Values	adaptable	60	M	P, T, O, D, M
32	Leading Values	work	90–120	M	P, T, O
33	Customer Values	work	185	M	T, O, D, M
34	Customer Service Values Survey	work	75	M	P, T
35	Cultural Interactions	work	70	M–H	P, O, D, M
36	What Is of Value?	general	15–30	M–H	P, D
37	Four Case Studies	work	50	M–H	P, T, O, D, M
38	Discovering Team Strengths and Values	adaptable	100	M–H	P, T, D, M
39	Your Values Meet the Team's Values	work	70–80	M–H	P, T, D, M
40	Simulation: Rockets and Sparklers	general	90	M–H	P, D, M
41	A Good Employee Is or Does	work	85–95	M–H	P, T, O, D, M
42	My Values	adaptable	60	M–H	P, T, D, M
43	What Do They Bring?	work	70–90	M–H	T, D
44	Behaviors I Find Difficult	work	90	M–H	P, D, M
45	Values Line	general	45–60	M–H	P, T, D
46	The Culture Compass	adaptable	90	M–H	P, O, D, M
47	Values of Conflict	general	90	M–H	P, T, D, M
48	Working with Values	work	80	M–H	P, T, O, D, M
49	Top Two	general	60	M–H	P, T, D, M
50	Survey Your Values	general	90	M–H	P, T, O, D, M
51	It's a Puzzle	general	40–60	H	P, T, O, D
52	Window to Our World	adaptable	75	H	M

Risk: L=Low, M=Medium, H=High

Purposes: P = Personal, T = Team, O = Organizational,
D = U.S. Diversity, M = Multinational

Introduction

Bend, flex or break the rules but never violate the values.
— King County Library System, 1997

Values are like fingerprints. Nobody's are the same, but you leave 'em all over everything you do.

— Elvis Presley

Values are deeply held beliefs that determine what is "good, right, and normal" and what is "bad, wrong, and abnormal" among members of a cultural group. Values, then, prescribe which ways of acting and being are perceived by a cultural group as better than others. Because of this and because values vary widely among cultural groups, they may—and often do—cause cross-cultural misunderstandings and conflict.

Values clashes occur frequently when people from different cultures interact. Even more important, differing cultural values exist not only country to country but also within corporations, organizations, universities, towns, ethnic groups, neighborhoods, and so on. In other words, we live with values differences every day and may be unaware when a misunderstanding or problem we encounter is based on such fundamental differences.

Consequently, most educators, trainers, and facilitators who explore intercultural and cross-cultural issues incorporate values into their planning. In designing our own academic classes and corporate workshops over the past three decades, we have often created our own values activities or modified those of others to shape an experience that fits a particular audience. In adapting or creating values activities, we have relied on the work of several well-known approaches to values. We'll take a brief look at these next because they form the framework on which ours and others' values activities are based.

What Do You Need to Know about Values?

The Terminal and Instrumental Approach. The terminal/instrumental values distinction was originally identified by Milton Rokeach. A terminal value is simply a goal. An instrumental value is the behavior used to achieve the goal. It is quite possible to share terminal values but exhibit different behaviors and equally possible to have different terminal values but exhibit the same behaviors.

For example, two people can share a terminal value of close family ties. One achieves this goal behaviorally by sharing a house with four generations of family; the other, by communicating with members of the family regularly, even though they are spread all over the world. The reverse is also true. Two people can share instrumental values (and behaviors); for example, they may both work very hard to earn as much money as possible. Their terminal values, however, may be quite different. For one individual, the goal is the security of having money in the bank and a college fund for the children; for the other the goal is to travel and experience as much of the world as possible.

So what's the point? The point is, of course, that we cannot observe people's terminal values or goals; we can only see their behavior (reflecting their instrumental values).

If I assume that because someone behaves differently from me that he or she has different goals and values, I could be wrong. If I assume that because that person behaves similarly we share the same goals and values, I could also be wrong. This is a critical distinction in developing cultural competency.

If my assumptions that others are "like me" or "not like me" are based on what I see, I may be led down the road to misperception, misunderstanding, negative judgment, and conflict. The only way I can know what goal-driven (terminal) values other people hold is to ask them, listen to them, observe them, and generate multiple interpretations for their behavior; in other words, get to know them.

Values Dimensions. A second primary framework regarding values that underlies our thinking when we adapt or create values activities is what is known as values dimensions, such as those identified by Florence Kluckhohn and Fred Strodtbeck, Geert Hofstede, and Fons Trompenaars, among others. These dimensions describe two opposite poles (e.g., individualism/collectivism, as mentioned in the example above) with an invisible line between them that represents the range of real-life value orientations for the same dimension. The task/relationship dimension is especially important for professionals and businesspeople working across cultures or, for that matter, instructors with task- and relationship-oriented students in the same class. The task-oriented students will prioritize an assigned paper over the needs of friends or family (or so the theory goes). The relationship-oriented student will consider picking up her cousin from the airport as more important than completing the assigned paper on time. The paper will, of course, be finished and submitted, though a bit late, after the cousin has been settled in. Or a task-oriented professional or businessperson might want to jump right into a job, identifying specific tasks, deadlines, and responsibilities, while a relationship-oriented person might first want to get to know the other participants on their team and have some "social" conversation before jumping into the job. Just how strongly each of them feels about this dimension determines their relative location along the continuum. Orientations toward task/relationship, hierarchy/equality, indirect/direct communication, and others can be plotted along the values dimensions continua as appropriate.

We have used many values continua in our discussions and activities with the idea that participants benefit from identifying where their own value orientation lies on any given continuum, then identifying where someone else might be on that same continuum, and finally identifying how to improve effectiveness across the difference. In other words, how might people modify their behavior temporarily to interact more effectively with each other?

The goals (terminal values) for both the student and the team members are, of course, to get the paper written and the job completed. Their behavioral approaches (reflecting instrumental values), however, are different. You can easily see how different instrumental values can lead to misperceptions and/or conflict, even when the end goal is the same. The task-oriented instructor, for instance, is likely to see the relationship-oriented student as lazy or unmotivated or even lacking respect for authority. The task-oriented team member often views the other team members as not serious, as wasting time, and as unfocused. Meanwhile, the relationship-oriented student and team member are likely to see the task-oriented people as cold, unfriendly, too serious, or rigid. But if both individuals understand that they are located at opposite ends of this particular continuum, it is much more likely that each can adapt his or her behavior to be more effective and reduce the potential for conflict.

Why Did We Create This Manual?

Although values activities appear scattered throughout numerous publications, are presented in workshops by their creators, and are tucked into packets for training sessions, we know of no available collection of values activities. Trainers, instructors, workshop leaders are often hard-pressed to locate a values activity that fits their objectives. We have pulled together this collection of 52 activities to make all of our lives easier, thus encouraging increased values exploration in all venues. We have collected and adapted existing values activities from many sources and have contributed a large number of our own to the book. No matter what your situation is, we hope you will find exercises here that will fit your objectives.

Who Is This Manual For?

As intercultural trainers and educators, we have used each of these activities in corporate or diversity training within workplace environments, in the United States as well as abroad. We have also used them in college, high school, and middle school classrooms. Given the diverse make up of high school and college classrooms, values activities can help students—and instructors—understand each other better and learn to negotiate values-based differences in a constructive manner. Because these activities are designed for adult learners, however, you may need to adapt them for high school and middle school students.

If you are an instructor of intermediate or advanced students for whom English is a second or foreign language (ESL/EFL), you may also find numerous activities in this manual that will help your students explore values-based issues and understand each other better both inside and outside their classrooms. You will also want to allow more time than allotted for each activity. Military personnel, missionaries, students preparing to study abroad, and members of organizations and groups of all kinds will benefit from understanding their own values and those of others with whom they will interact.

In short, anyone who is interested in becoming more effective with others will find much of value in these pages.

What Will You Get from This Manual?

You will find not only a wide variety of activities on values exploration, but also two mechanisms (see "How to Use This Manual" below) for helping you choose the right activity for your situation. Each activity includes all that you need in order to conduct it:

1. *Time Required* to complete the activity, broken down according to each segment of the activity
2. *Objectives* for the activities presented in an easy-to-read list
3. *Materials* required for facilitating the activity
4. *Process* (clear, numbered instructions for leading the activity)
5. *Debriefing Questions* that will make this most-important aspect of any values activity easy for you *(Note: We have purposely written these questions to be quite general because we have found that asking a few germane questions generates rich discussion and meaningful learning.)*
6. *Debriefing Conclusions*, those basic truths we hope will be identified by the participants during the activity and the debriefing (If they do not identify all of the conclusions reached during the debriefing, you may add to our list to summarize points that may have been overlooked.)

In a few activities we have provided what we label "Additional Processes," "Optional Processes," "Optional Debriefing questions," and so on. These are offered as alternative suggestions depending on time allotment or needs of the participants. Notes made in italics are "behind-the-scenes" comments for you, not for the participants.

You will also find in Appendix F detailed information about choosing appropriate activities for your participants based on comfort level. The Resource Bibliography rounds out the manual with readings on the intercultural theory that underlies values work and additional training materials that include but are not limited to values exploration.

How to Use This Manual

Choosing the right activities for your particular situation from a book of 52 of them can be a time-consuming task, time that many of you would far rather spend preparing an activity than searching for one. We have supplied a chart called "General Classification of Activities"; if you study this chart rather than flipping through the exercises, you may save time and avoid choosing an inappropriate activity for your group.

General Classification of Activities. This chart (pages viii and ix) categorizes all 52 activities by context, time required, risk level, and purpose.

Context: The activities fall into three categories: general, work, and adaptable. General activities can be used to explore values in any setting. Work-oriented activities are to be used in any context where people are working together. Adaptable activities are designed for work-related groups but can quite easily be adapted for a general audience.

Time: Listings are in total minutes required to complete the activity, including the debriefing. We don't recommend that you try to skimp on the time allotments, especially debriefing, which is the most essential and valuable aspect of an activity.

Risk Level: It is difficult to gauge the level of risk involved in an activity because what is of medium risk for one person may be quite threatening to another. Risk level is broken down in this manual as follows: low, low-medium, medium, medium-high, and high.

There are three participant characteristics that help determine risk level: developmental stage or intellectual ability, emotional comfort level, and perceived appropriateness of self-disclosure. Low-risk activities are most appropriate for participants who are in early stages of intercultural understanding and for inexperienced trainers. For a discussion of this subject, see Appendix F, "Choosing Appropriate Activities for Participants' Developmental Stages."

Purpose: This category refers to the type of values being explored. Personal (P) activities allow participants to increase self-awareness by exploring their own cultural values. Team (T) activities are particularly useful for exploring values that have an impact on team interactions and effectiveness. Organizational (O) activities take a broader view of an organization's implicit and explicit cultural values. Multinational (M) activities are those we have found useful with groups that include participants from a diverse range of national backgrounds, and domestic diversity (D) activities we use primarily with diverse groups within the United States.

Debriefing Approach

In addition to probing specifically about values, the debriefing questions at the end of most activities are designed with David Kolb's four learning styles in mind (see page xvi). Thus, you will find a question at the end of each activity that asks about feelings, thoughts, observations, actions, and application as well as about values.

You are welcome to add more debriefing questions if you like, but we caution less-experienced trainers against using too many questions during the debriefing. Asking a few germane questions is more likely to generate rich discussion and more meaningful learning. Additionally, we caution inexperienced trainers to provide sufficient time for debriefing because, as mentioned earlier, this is where much of the learning takes place.

A Note about Adult Learning Styles

David A. Kolb's (1985) approach to learning styles served as a framework and guide for our development of these activities. Kolb discusses four types of learning preferences: (a) concrete experience, (b) reflective observation, (c) abstract conceptualization, and (d) active experimentation. We have attempted to include as many types of learning preferences in each activity and its debriefing as fit the activity conceptually. Following is a brief description and example of each type of learning preference.

Concrete Experience requires learning by relating to other people and identifying feelings. Small-group discussions regarding personal experiences and feelings about an issue make use of this preference.

Reflective Observation requires people to observe what goes on around them, think about what they have seen, and explore their observations from a range of perspectives. Even though this preference is the most difficult to address in training because of the length of time it can take, it can be included through a journal-writing activity or by the debriefing questions asked.

Abstract Conceptualization involves systematic planning, logical analysis, and intellectual understanding of a situation or theory. This is addressed through lectures or problem-solving activities such as case studies.

Active Experimentation is the "doing" preference and includes completing self-assessment instruments and participating in simulations and role plays, among other activities. Participants often remember active experimentation as the most enjoyable part of a class or workshop. Because people learn differently, however, "doing" cannot be the entire focus of the training. It is also important for you to know that these activities can be high risk and may not be appropriate based on your participants' comfort with risk, and your own level of experience.

While many will ask, or demand, that your training design be primarily experiential—a trend in both corporate and educational settings today in the United States—we caution you to balance all four styles. Too much "doing" can result in little or no understanding of the underlying reason that a behavior or action may or may not be effective cross-culturally; too much thinking can result in participants being bored or not learning how to apply the information.

1

Cultural Values

Time Required

35 minutes (5 minutes to brief, 10 minutes for the activity, 20 minutes to debrief)

Objectives

1. To clarify the differences between universal, cultural, and personal values
2. To illustrate that values fall across a continuum, with cultural values as the midpoint between the poles of universal and personal values
3. To prove that those who say "people are all alike" (universal values) and those who say we are "all unique individuals" (personal values) are denying that culture is an important influence on the values we hold
4. To provide information regarding the dangers of overgeneralizing cultural values

Materials

- The Cultural Values Worksheet

Process

1. Define the different values:
   - People everywhere share *global values*, for example, respect.
   - People within a specific cultural group share *cultural values* that are not necessarily shared by all cultural groups; for example, competition.
   - Individuals hold *personal values* that are unique to each individual; for example, artistic skill development. A personal value may be shared by a number of people in a culture, but it would not be considered a cultural value unless *most* people in the culture shared that value.
2. Inform participants that values may fit into one, two, or all three categories.
3. Ask participants to complete the "Cultural Values" worksheet.

4. After everyone has completed the worksheet, review the items together as a large group. Focus discussion on those items that people did not agree on and ask participants to explain their choices.

Debriefing Questions

1. What happened? What was easiest to do? Hardest? Why?
2. How did you feel about completing this sheet? Why?
3. What would you conclude about values from this experience?
4. What did you learn?
5. How can you apply what you've learned?

Debriefing Conclusions

1. While some values are global, there are also many cultural and individual differences in values.
2. We all belong to the global human race and to specific cultural groups, and we each have individual personalities; our values come from all three.
3. While some behavior may be more prevalent within certain cultures, personal preferences and differences exist in every culture.

Based on information from *Figuring Foreigners Out* by Craig Storti.*

---

* For this book and others cited herein, please refer to the Resource Bibliography for complete publishing information.

Cultural Values Worksheet

Write a *G* for those items that illustrate global values. Write a *C* for those items that exemplify cultural values, and write a *P* for those items indicating personal values.

_____ 1. Sleeping with a bedroom window open

_____ 2. Running from a dangerous animal

_____ 3. Considering snakes to be "evil"

_____ 4. Assigning a higher value to male children than to female children

_____ 5. Respecting elders and seeking their counsel

_____ 6. Learning one's native language

_____ 7. Developing artistic skills

_____ 8. Seeing family as important

_____ 9. Eating at certain times

_____ 10. Considering competing and winning important

_____ 11. Enjoying the poetry of Rainer Maria Rilke

_____ 12. Calling a waiter with a hissing sound

_____ 13. Surrounding oneself with the color blue

_____ 14. Seeking harmony in everything one does

_____ 15. Feeling sad at the death of one's mother

_____ 16. Seeking physical safety

_____ 17. Choosing a religion or form of spirituality to practice

_____ 18. Being calm and self-controlled at all times

_____ 19. Eating no dairy products

Adapted from an activity in *Figuring Foreigners Out* by Craig Storti.

Cultural Values Answer Sheet

   P   1. Sleeping with a bedroom window open

   G   2. Running from a dangerous animal

   C   3. Considering snakes to be "evil"

   C   4. Assigning a higher value to male children than to female children

   C   5. Respecting elders and seeking their counsel

   G   6. Learning one's native language

   P   7. Developing artistic skills

   G   8. Seeing family as important

  P/C   9. Eating at certain times

   C   10. Considering competing and winning important

   P   11. Enjoying the poetry of Rainer Maria Rilke

   C   12. Calling a waiter with a hissing sound

   P   13. Surrounding oneself with the color blue

   C   14. Seeking harmony in everything one does

   P   15. Feeling sad at the death of one's mother

   G   16. Seeking physical safety

   C   17. Choosing a religion or form of spirituality to practice

  P/C   18. Being calm and self-controlled at all times

   C   19. Eating no dairy products

Adapted from an activity in *Figuring Foreigners Out* by Craig Storti.

2

A "Jolt" of Reality

Time Required

8–15 minutes (3–5 minutes for the activity, 5–10 minutes to debrief)

Objectives

1. To illustrate how we filter information and form assumptions based on experience and cultural values
2. To encourage participants to reexamine their assumptions and to avoid automatic (knee-jerk) reactions
3. To demonstrate how our behaviors (action/reaction) are often influenced by cultural values or filters

Materials

- None

Process

1. Ask the participants to stand and find a partner. Direct partners to face each other, place their feet firmly on the floor, and then raise both hands and place them palm to palm at shoulder height.
2. Now tell participants that to win at this activity, they must make the other person move his or her feet—within 30 seconds. Start the timing. *(Note: Most participants will use brute force to push each other. Some may try to negotiate or bribe the other person to move. A few may stop pushing and let the other person's momentum propel him or her forward.)*
3. After 30 seconds stop the activity and ask a few participants to share some of the strategies they used to get the other person to move.
4. Ask for a volunteer. Assume the face-to-face, palm-to-palm position. Whisper to the other person, "Let's dance." Hum a tune and move your feet together.
5. The participants will probably protest that this is cheating. Remind them that the directions were simply to get the other person to move his or her feet within the 30–second time frame. There were no restrictions on moving your own feet or on communicating. Ask participants who won.

Debriefing Questions

1. Describe what happened. (When you hear interpretations, such as "She tried to bribe me," rather than descriptions like "She offered me something," ask the participants to describe behaviors only.)
2. How did you feel about how you behaved? Your partner's behaviors? The outcome?
3. What values were behind the different strategies people used?
4. What did you learn from the activity itself and from the "dance" strategy?
5. How can this learning be applied?

Debriefing Conclusions

1. We tend to filter information, form assumptions based on our own experience and values, and then act according to these assumptions. Cultural values such as cooperation, competition, individualism, and collectivism are demonstrated in this kind of activity.
2. Assumptions and knee-jerk reactions can prevent us from exploring alternative behaviors.
3. Cultural values such as individualism and competition may result in conflict and block win-win solutions.
4. Meeting force with force is almost always futile.

Adapted from an activity presented by Sivasailam Thiagarajan at The Summer Institute for Intercultural Communication, 2000.

3

Let's Draw a House

Time Required
20 minutes (2 minutes to set up; 3 minutes for the activity; 15 minutes for debriefing)

Objectives
1. To experience leader and follower patterns
2. To demonstrate relational and task-oriented perspectives
3. To discuss personal and cultural influences on behavior

Materials
- Blank paper
- A pen or pencil for each pair

Process
1. Ask participants to find a partner. Explain that this activity works best if their partners are people they don't know. Give each pair one sheet of paper and one pencil.
2. Inform participants that, without talking, each two-person team is to cooperatively draw a house. Both people on each team must hold the pencil during the entire activity. After two or three minutes, ask the teams to stop. They can show their house to those near them or hold them up for the group to see.

There are usually three types of houses that are drawn:
1. "Primary school" houses, where either both people visualized the house in the same way or one person drew and the other was a "hitchhiker"
2. Houses that look like two houses, where one person started to feel guilty about taking control and let the other person complete the drawing
3. Drawings that don't resemble houses at all but rather aimlessly wandering lines, where each person tried to help the other; either no one took control or both people were competing and neither would give up control

---

3. Encourage different teams to share what the experience was like for them.
4. Explore the individualism/group and hierarchy/equity value orientations.

Debriefing Questions
1. What values might influence the different experiences?
2. What differences in task and relationship orientations did you discover?
3. How might the spirit of cooperation or competition affect performance?
4. How might misunderstandings arise between those having the individualist and group orientations? Between the hierarchy and equity orientations?
5. How might this apply to real-life situations?
6. How might culture influence behavior (visualization of "house," task/relationship orientation, etc.)?

Adapted from an activity by Paul B. Pedersen in *Intercultural Sourcebook: Cross-Cultural Training Methods,* vol. 2, edited by Sandra M. Fowler and Monica G. Mumford.

Time Values

Time Required

60–75 minutes (5 minutes for completion of handout; 25 minutes for small-group discussion; 30–45 minutes for large-group discussion and debriefing)

Objectives

1. To identify how values are revealed in cultural sayings or idioms
2. To learn how the dominant cultural values regarding time affect work behaviors

   Note: This activity is to be used with groups in work situations so that any suggested changes that come up in the activity can be implemented. Typically, this will be supervisors or managers. In organizations that value—and utilize—employee suggestions, this can also be used with employees. Do not use it with employees if there has not been a process identified for hearing and implementing employee suggestions.

Materials

- Time Sayings Handout

Process

1. Distribute the "Time Sayings" handout to all participants.
2. Ask people to individually select the five sayings that most represent how time is perceived and used in their organization. They may add sayings to the list if they wish.
3. Ask the participants to form small groups of 3–5 people and then (a) come to agreement about which five sayings are most representative of how time is perceived and used in their organization and (b) identify specific behaviors within the organization that support their selections.
4. Then ask small groups to identify, based on their selection of sayings and behaviors, whether their organization is oriented to past, present, or future time, whether the pace is slow or fast, and how the organization's time orientation and pace do or do not serve it well.

5. Ask a representative of each small group to report its discussion. In those areas where there are differences between groups, discuss why these differences might have occurred.
6. In the large group, have participants discuss how the organization's time orientation and pace impact the following:
   - *Planning* (determining objectives, selecting priorities and work to be done)
   - *Organizing* (dividing the work into manageable functions)
   - *Motivating* (encouraging people to perform in a desired way)
   - *Innovating* (dealing with change)
   - *Delegating* (giving people responsibilities and authority)
7. Ask the group to identify any strategies for modifying behaviors when the time orientation or pacing does not serve the organization well.

Debriefing Questions

1. What happened? How easy was it to come to agreement on the sayings in the small groups? How consistent was the perception of the organization's values about time across your small groups? Were any of the disagreements based on individual departmental differences or role responsibilities?
2. How did you feel during the discussions? Why?
3. What values—individual and organizational—arose in the discussions in either the small groups or the larger group?
4. What did you learn?
5. How can you apply what you learned to your workplace?

Debriefing Conclusions

1. Individuals and organizations have orientations to time that are reflected in cultural sayings.
2. Orientations to time affect the way business is conducted...often without awareness.
3. An organization's orientation to time and its pacing can both benefit and get in the way of effectiveness.
4. Orientation to time can vary in different areas of an organization based on job function or responsibilities.

Adapted from an activity in *Training for the Cross-Cultural Mind* by Pierre Casse.

Time Sayings Handout

Respect other people's time.

Budget your time.

Have a good time.

Time is life.

Take your time.

Use your waiting time.

Your time will come.

Be on time.

Don't waste your time.

It's time consuming.

The time of your life.

Find the time.

Make the most of your time.

Running out of time.

Time is money.

Save your time.

You'll do better next time.

good timing

killing time

beating time

in the nick of time

5

Age Case Study

```
┌─────────────┐
│   Work      │
│             │
│    L        │
│             │
│   P, D      │
└─────────────┘
```

Time Required

60 minutes (10 minutes for reading the case individually, 20 minutes for small-group discussion, 30 minutes for debriefing)

Objectives

1. To learn some values and behavior differences between generations
2. To apply information about generational values and norms to a workplace case study

Materials

- Case Study: Age Differences Handout

Process

1. Provide each participant with the case study "Age Differences" handout and give the group ten minutes to read it.
2. Provide participants with additional information about generational differences as appropriate (see the three handouts in Activity 17, "Generational Values," pages 63–66).
3. Place participants in small groups of 4–6 and ask them to discuss what actions Sandy should take.
4. Bring the groups back together and ask them to share their solutions, looking for areas of commonality and difference. Where differences occur, explore why groups (or individuals within groups) took different approaches and look for how each approach could be helpful.

Debriefing Questions

1. What happened during the small-group discussion? What conclusions were easiest for the group? Hardest? Why?
2. How did you feel about the discussion? Why? Did any individuals have more influence than others in the discussion? Why?
3. What generational values came into play in the case study?
4. What strategies might Sandy employ to motivate C Team?
5. What personal values made this activity easiest or hardest? Why?
6. What did you learn?
7. How can you apply what you learned to everyday work life?

Debriefing Conclusions

1. Generational norms are not stereotypes—please don't use them that way.
2. Personal experiences and role responsibilities in the workplace can affect the way we respond to this case study—and to real work situations.
3. Understanding generational differences can provide us with an additional resource as we seek to resolve work situations and to reduce cross-generational conflicts.
4. There is no one "right" answer to any work situation. Rather, collaborating across differences, including generational differences, can help us identify a range of options.

Age Differences Handout

Sandy Katzenbacker has just learned that due to a merger and reorganization, she and all of the other midlevel managers in her company must reapply for their jobs. Sandy has survived downsizing before because she always meets or exceeds her sales targets—until this year, that is.

Sandy manages five sales teams. All but one of those teams has failed to meet its goals this year. Sandy has tried many standard management methods to boost the lagging team's performance: pep talks, cajoling, challenging, and the like. Now, with the announced reapplication process a little more than a month away, the pressure is on to get the nonproducers turned around. Sandy has decided to examine the strengths and weaknesses of the teams, beginning with the highest- and lowest-performing teams—A Team and C Team.

A Team (the best performers) is made up of people who thrive on competition. Some members are high achievers. Turnover is almost nonexistent. All members seem to understand that they could not do as well working alone. They work hard and put in the long hours necessary to continue their success. Politically, they are sharp. As a team they know how to look good for upper management and how to make Sandy look good too. They are well networked throughout the company and often spend off-hours doing things together.

C Team is not producing at all. Its members seem to be constantly fighting among themselves. They often fight with members of the other teams, too. The team has high turnover, and the changes in membership don't bring about improvements in performance. Their battles seem to revolve around work assignments, hours worked, technology, and interpersonal relations. Two new members are real "computer geeks." They have no patience with the older members of the team, who seem to them to be reluctant to "move into the twenty-first century." The

two geeks are notorious for coming in late, leaving early, and refusing overtime. They don't follow directions, which generates a variety of reactions from other team members. In addition, others complain about their rudeness, defined as typing e-mails when others are trying to have a serious conversation with them.

This pair complains that some team members are too rigid, wanting to do everything by the book. They (the older members) want all transactions to be in person or by telephone and refuse to leave or return voice messages. They also do only what they are told and offer no ideas for doing things differently. Their motto seems to be "If it ain't broke, don't fix it." These older, "rigid" folks always show up on time and go the extra mile when necessary.

The remaining members are good individual performers but are judgmental and intolerant of others. They bring complaints directly to Sandy instead of to their team leader, alleging that the newest team members have a poor work ethic, terrible interpersonal skills, and a "What's in it for me?" attitude. They also complain that these new workers always want to change things faster than anyone could adapt to while the older workers want no change at all.

As a first step toward solving these problems, Sandy meets with the leaders of both teams simultaneously. Her assessment causes the A Team leader to gloat and the C Team leader to explode. "It's no wonder A does it right. They're Boomers. You're a Boomer, too, but I'm not, and my team is different."

Sandy realizes that what C Team's leader is saying is true. Nearly all of the members of A are in their forties and fifties, and they generally do what they're told and have years of experience with the company. On the other hand, C's members are a mix of generations. Those who hate technology are generally the oldest members of the team, while those who love technology and feel most comfortable using it are the youngest.

What would you suggest that Sandy do?

Adapted from *Generations at Work: Managing the Clash of Veterans, Boomers, Xers, and Nexters,* copyright (C) 2000, Performance Research Associates, Inc., Ron Zemke, Claire Raines, Bob Filipczak. AMACOM, a division of American Managment Association, New York, NY. Used by permission of the publisher. All rights reserved.

6

A Value to D. I. E. For

Time Required

30 minutes (5 minutes to describe objects 10 minutes to teach D.I.E.;
15 minutes in small groups; 30 minutes to debrief)

Objectives

1. To clarify the differences between description (D), interpretation
   (I), and evaluation (E)
2. To demonstrate that people tend to begin with interpretation and
   evaluation, rarely description
3. To demonstrate how personal experiences and cultural values influence our interpretation and evaluation
4. To provide practice in describing, stressing the importance of observation

Materials

- 1 or 2 ambiguous objects
- Flipchart
- At least one picture from a different cultural setting, either national
  or workplace, for every five members

Process

1. Introduce an ambiguous object (kitchen gadget, tool from another
   country, etc.), something you feel confident that participants will
   not have seen before. Pass the object around and ask participants,
   "Tell me something about it." Chart responses on a sheet of paper
   in three unlabeled columns representing Description, Interpretation,
   and Evaluation.
2. Present the concept of D.I.E.

Description	What I see	It is metal. It is gold.
Interpretation	What I think about what I see	It is jewelry.
Evaluation	What I feel about what I see	It is beautiful.

3. Ask participants to generate alternative interpretations and evaluations.
4. Place participants in groups of 5 and give each group a picture from
   a different cultural setting. Ask the groups to discuss the picture
   using the D.I.E. technique: describe, interpret, and evaluate.

5. Ask the groups to show their pictures and share their responses.

Debriefing Questions

1. What happened? What was most difficult? Easiest? Why?
2. How did you feel when you were asked to describe without interpreting or evaluating?
3. How might personal or cultural values influence the interpretation or evaluation?
4. What did you learn?
5. How can you use what you learned in your everyday life?

Debriefing Conclusions

1. People tend to jump to interpretations and evaluations without first describing and entertaining alternative interpretations and evaluations.
2. Our interpretations and evaluations are based on our own experience and cultural learning.
3. When we can first describe, then look for alternative interpretations and evaluations, we are likely to be more accurate and more effective cross-culturally.

Optional Process

1. Teach the participants D.I.E. as an effective communication tool. Place D = Describe, I = Interpret, and E = Evaluate on a flipchart. Ask people which of these we typically do when we first observe someone else's behavior. They will probably say "evaluate" or "interpret." Point out that if you first interpret and then evaluate—or first evaluate and then interpret—you are doing so from your own perspective. A more effective way to learn about others and avoid misinterpretations is to describe the others' behavior objectively and then ask them to interpret it for you from their perspective. Then you can evaluate it with both your perspective and theirs in mind.

2. Give an illustration that makes sense for the setting in which you are using the activity. For example, I might dislike a co-worker (evaluation) and consider her rude (interpretation) because she doesn't greet me in the morning (description). I might say to her one day, "Every morning when I pass you in the hall and say good morning, you do not respond. Help me understand what that is about." *(Note: The tone with which you ask the question is important—be sure it is neutral and information seeking, not judgmental.)* She might respond by saying, "Wow! I hadn't even noticed that. I begin my morning by trying to get focused on my most important tasks for the day, and when I do that, I often don't notice anything around me. I am really sorry. I certainly never intended to be rude or to offend you." Might I now interpret and evaluate the behavior differently? Give the participants time to respond.

3. Conduct an unrehearsed role play with your cotrainer, a teacher, or a participant by spontaneously asking him or her for something. For

example, ask him (or her) for the D.I.E. handouts you requested. Play this out for 1 or 2 minutes, insisting that you gave him the handouts and asking him to search his briefcase or his materials, and so on. Finally, give up (throw your arms up) and say, "That's okay, I'll just use the flipchart."

Note: You can prepare someone for this, but it needs to look spontaneous and authentic. If you don't have a cotrainer and use a participant, be sure to use someone who will not be embarrassed or offended. And be sure to thank that person when you are finished for allowing you to "play" with her or him.

4. Turn to the flipchart and draw a line down the middle. Ask the participants, "What did you just see?" After every two or three responses, repeat "What did you just see?" Write down their responses, with interpretations and evaluations on one side and descriptions on the other side. You will rarely get many descriptions. Most of the responses will be, for instance, "surprise," "disorganization," "irritation," "frustration," "blame," and so forth. Keep asking the question until you have a substantial list.

5. Point out that you have interpretations and evaluations on one side and descriptions on the other. Point out that even though you have just taught them a new tool, they still jumped to interpretations and evaluations when you asked them what they saw. Acknowledge that D.I.E. is not easy to use but that it is a critical tool for cross-cultural effectiveness: I cannot know what your behavior means unless I ask you. Urge the participants to practice using D.I.E. over the next few days and assure them that it will get easier as they do so.

Note: If the group has used more descriptive language than interpretations and evaluations, acknowledge it, congratulate them, and encourage them to continue using descriptions as often as possible.

The D.I.E. activity was created some time ago and is now considered public domain. This particular activity was adapted from Milton and Janet Bennett's version, Intercultural Communication Institute, Portland, Oregon.

7

Role Models

Time Required

55–70 minutes (5–10 minutes for individual work; 20 minutes for small-group discussions; 10–20 minutes for small-group reports; 20 minutes for debriefing)

Objectives

1. To identify personal role models
2. To describe behaviors of role models
3. To explore the values that role model behaviors symbolize

Materials

• Paper and pencil for each participant

Process

1. Ask each participant to identify 3–5 of his or her personal role models and a few adjectives describing each one. These role models may come from any time in history, any walk of life. They may be fictional or nonfictional. (*Note: It may be helpful for the trainer to provide some personal examples.*)
2. Place participants into groups of 3–5 people and ask them to share their lists of names and accompanying adjectives, writing them down as they go. After each person has shared his or her names and adjectives, ask the group to discuss the cultural values that may be reflected by those adjectives. Ask each group to choose 2–3 role models to share with the large group.
3. Reconvene the larger group and ask each small group to share the role models they discussed and the behaviors and values they used to describe their role models.

Debriefing Questions

1. What happened? Why? Did people in your small group have some of the same role models? The same behaviors or values? What do you think that tells us about culture? How easy or difficult was it for your small group to identify which two or three role models to present to the larger group? Why?

2. How did you feel as you were identifying your role models? As you shared them with others? As you listened to others' choices?
3. What values made this activity difficult or easy? What national values are represented in the role models you identified? Were there more people of any one group identified, for example, gender, race/ethnicity, occupation? What cultural or personal values might explain this?
4. What did you learn? Did the discussion give you any new ways to think about role models? Based on this discussion, who might you be a role model for?
5. How could you apply information from this experience to your everyday life?

Debriefing Conclusions

1. Individual role models are based on both personal and cultural values.
2. Individuals from the same culture will often have similar role models.
3. Describing role models can be a rich, nonthreatening source for understanding behavior that is valued within a culture.

8

Saying It Makes It So

Time Required

60–75 minutes (30 minutes for small groups; 15 minutes to report; 15–30 minutes for debriefing)

Objectives

1. To identify values that are implied by common expressions
2. To explore the tacit ways that culture is transferred from generation to generation

Materials

- Saying It Makes It So Handout
- Paper, pencils
- Flipchart (optional)

Process

1. Place participants in groups of 4–6 people. Provide each person with the "Saying It Makes It So" handout. Give the groups approximately 30 minutes to do the following:
   - Add any expressions that group members remember from their childhood.
   - Identify where people learned these expressions.
   - Identify the implicit values being taught by each expression.
   - Discuss whether there are differences within the group based on cultural experiences including geography, gender, race/ethnicity, and so on.
2. Returning to the larger group, ask small groups to share the values they identified for each expression and any differences they might have identified within their group. If time allows, record these values on a flipchart so the group can see the similarities and differences.

Debriefing Questions

1. Were there differences in the expressions people knew or remembered? What do you think these differences are based on? From whom did you learn these expressions? How early in life?

2. How do you feel about these expressions and the implicit or explicit values they express?
3. What values did your group members demonstrate as they participated? Which values were most commonly held? Why do you think that is?
4. Were there expressions you had never heard before? Why do you think that is?
5. How could you apply information from this experience to your everyday life?

Debriefing Conclusions

1. The values of a culture are often passed on by the implicit and explicit use of common expressions.
2. Expressions can serve as a tool to better understand tacit cultural values.

Additional Process

Note: This process could be very helpful in preparing people to visit or work internationally.

3. Following Step 2 (reporting back to the larger group regarding U.S. cultural sayings), provide participants with sayings common to the country they are preparing to study or visit and have them identify the values implicit in the sayings.
4. Ask participants to identify differences in the values represented in U.S. expressions and those in the expressions of the chosen country, as represented in the sayings provided.
5. Ask participants to identify behavioral modifications they might want to make to be most effective in the chosen country based on the identified value differences.

Optional Process

Note: This process is likely to take longer because people are being asked to generate their own lists of expressions. This will be a much richer process, however, if there is a mix of cultures represented in the group.

1. Ask each person to write down any expressions or idioms they remember from their own experiences—both past and current.
2. Place participants in groups of 4–6. Have the small groups identify common expressions and unique expressions, identifying the source of the latter (e.g., nationality, geography, gender, race/ethnicity, etc.). Have the group identify the values implicit in each saying. Ask one person in each group to write this information down.
3. After participants return to the larger group, ask each small group to report the expressions that were shared by most people in their group and those that were unique, including the values implicit in each saying and the source of the expression. If time allows, record the values on a flipchart for comparison.

Adapted from activities in *Developing Intercultural Awarenesss: A Cross-Cultural Training Handbook* by L. Robert Kohls and John M. Knight.

Saying It Makes It So Handout

1. Make hay while the sun shines.
2. Keep your ear to the ground.
3. Fly by the seat of your pants.
4. Easy as rolling off a log.
5. Dot your i's and cross your t's.
6. The early bird catches the worm.
7. Wrong side of the tracks.
8. Roll with the punches.
9. Can't see the forest for the trees.
10. Throw your hat into the ring.
11. Don't make waves.
12. There is more than one way to skin a cat.
13. Dyed in the wool.
14. Shape up or ship out.
15. Don't take any wooden nickels.
16. Save for a rainy day.
17. Right off the bat.
18. Don't cry over spilt milk.
19. Cleanliness is next to godliness.
20. A penny saved is a penny earned.
21. Waste not; want not.
22. It's not whether you win or lose; it's how you play the game.
23. God helps those who help themselves.
24. You've made your bed; now lie in it.
25. Early to bed, early to rise, makes a man healthy, wealthy and wise.
26. Time is money.
27. Children should be seen but not heard.
28. A woman's place is in the home.
29. Fish or cut bait.
30. Go along for the ride.

Organizations in Cultural Perspective

<table>
<tr><td>Work</td></tr>
<tr><td>L</td></tr>
<tr><td>P, T, O, M</td></tr>
</table>

Time Required

60 minutes (5 minutes on individual work; 15 minutes to contrast worksheet with handout; 40 minutes for discussion and debriefing)

Objectives

1. To identify the ways that cultural values influence the structure of the organization and the expectations of managers and leaders
2. To examine the implications of individual and national differences for cross-cultural managers
3. To discuss the value and challenge of individual and national differences within an organization
4. To generate suggestions to enhance cross-cultural effectiveness

   Note: This activity is intended for managers working in organizations that have an international mix of managers or leaders. It will be of maximum benefit for a group of international managers working in the same organization.

Materials

- Organizations in Cultural Perspective Worksheet
- International Responses Handout
- Overhead projector and overheads (optional; see Process, Step 2)

Process

1. Ask participants to individually answer the six statements on the "Organizations in Cultural Perspective" worksheet.
2. Distribute the "International Responses" handout. Referring to the international responses to the questions, ask participants to compare their own responses with those of others from their own country and with those from other countries. (*Note: The international responses can be shared by creating transparencies and/or photocopying the material and distributing it as a handout.*)
3. Discuss both individual and national differences, asking how those differences can benefit their organization and how they might create challenges.
4. Discuss what members of the organization can do that will maximize

the benefits and minimize the challenges of their differences.

Debriefing Questions

1. What happened during this discussion? In what areas was there the greatest agreement? Disagreement?
2. How did you feel as you (a) read over the statements, (b) made your choice, (c) and learned of the responses from managers in other cultures?
3. What differences in cultural values were identified? Which actions or behaviors were helpful to you in the discussion of the differences? Were there actions or behaviors that interfered with your group participation? What values of yours got in your way?
4. What did you learn?
5. How can you apply this information to your work life?

Debriefing Conclusions

1. Cultural values influence expectations and perceptions of the manager's or leader's role and of appropriate organizational structures.
2. The differences in expectations/perceptions can be an advantage to an organization's effectiveness. These same differences can also present challenges to organizational effectiveness.
3. Recognition of the differences provides an opportunity to maximize the benefits of differences and minimize the challenges within an organization.

Adapted from research reported in "Reinventing Management at the Cross-Roads of Culture" by André Laurent.

Organizations in Cultural Perspective Worksheet

For each of the six statements, please circle the response that best represents your feeling (SA = strongly agree; A= agree; N = neutral; D = disagree; SD = strongly disagree).

1. Most managers have a clear notion of what we call an organizational structure.	SA	A	N	D	SD
2. The main reason for having a hierarchical structure is so that everyone knows who has authority over whom.	SA	A	N	D	SD
3. The manager of tomorrow will need to be primarily a negotiator.	SA	A	N	D	SD
4. Most managers would achieve better results if their roles were *less* precisely defined.	SA	A	N	D	SD
5. It is important for a manager to have precise answers to most of the questions subordinates may raise about their work.	SA	A	N	D	SD
6. An organizational structure in which certain subordinates have two direct bosses should be avoided at all costs.	SA	A	N	D	SD

Adapted from research reported in "Reinventing Management at the Cross-Roads of Culture" by André Laurent.

International Responses Handout

1. Most managers have a clear notion of what we call an organizational structure.

Country	Sample Size (772 managers)	Percent that Agree (Approx.)
Denmark	54	78
France	219	47
Germany	72	69
Great Britain	190	77
Italy	32	39
Netherlands	42	63
Sweden	50	70
Switzerland	63	62
United States	50	58

2. The main reason for having a hierarchical structure is so that everyone knows who has authority over whom.

Country	Sample Size (772 managers)	Percent that Agree (Approx.)
Denmark	54	35
France	219	45
Germany	72	24
Great Britain	190	38
Italy	32	50
Netherlands	42	38
Sweden	50	26
Switzerland	63	25
United States	50	18

3. The manager of tomorrow will need to be primarily a negotiator.

Country	Sample Size (772 managers)	Percent that Agree (Approx.)
Denmark	54	63
France	219	86
Germany	72	52
Great Britain	190	61
Italy	32	66
Netherlands	42	71
Sweden	50	66
Switzerland	63	41
United States	50	50

4. Most managers would achieve better results if their roles were *less* precisely defined.

Country	Sample Size (772 managers)	Percent that Agree (Approx.)
Denmark	54	33
France	219	28
Germany	72	26
Great Britain	190	32
Italy	32	31
Netherlands	42	48
Sweden	50	50
Switzerland	63	29
United States	50	46

5. It is important for a manager to have precise answers to most of the questions subordinates may raise about their work.

Country	Sample Size (772 managers)	Percent that Agree (Approx.)
Denmark	54	23
France	219	53
Germany	72	46
Great Britain	190	27
Italy	32	66
Netherlands	42	17
Sweden	50	10
Switzerland	63	38
United States	50	18

6. An organizational structure in which certain subordinates have two direct bosses should be avoided at all costs.

Country	Sample Size (772 managers)	Percent that Agree (Approx.)
Denmark	54	69
France	219	83
Germany	72	79
Great Britain	190	74
Italy	32	81
Netherlands	42	60
Sweden	50	64
Switzerland	63	76
United States	50	54

Adapted from research reported in "Reinventing Management at the Cross-Roads of Culture" by André Laurent.

10

Cross-Cultural Values

General

L

P, T, D, M

Time Required
60 minutes (5 minutes for individual work; 20 minutes for small-group discussion; 35 minutes for large-group discussion and debriefing)

Objectives
1. To explore the ways that cultural values differ in relation to human nature, the natural world, time, activity, and relationships
2. To examine the implications of these basic value differences
3. To generate suggestions for enhancing cross-cultural understanding

Materials
- Cross-Cultural Values Worksheet
- Flipchart and tape for hanging
- Marking pens

Process
1. Ask participants to complete the "Cross-Cultural Values" worksheet.
2. Place participants in groups of 3–5, then ask them to compare their responses, discuss any differences, and come to consensus on a group choice.
3. Ask each small group to report its responses to each question, charting the responses on a flipchart.

   Note: Questions 1 and 2 are designed to measure values regarding human nature; questions 3 and 4 measure values regarding the relationship of people to nature; questions 5 and 6, time; questions 7 and 8, activity; and questions 9 and 10, relationships. Thus, there are five value sets.

4. Ask the large group to discuss how different responses to any of these five value sets might affect perceptions and potential cooperation or conflict. Explore what steps might be taken to minimize misperceptions or conflict resulting from differences.

Debriefing Questions

1. What happened? Where did your groups come to agreement easily? Disagreement?
2. How did you feel as you (a) made your individual choices (b) shared your choices within the group, (c) worked toward consensus within the group, and (d) discussed the differences and similarities in the larger group?
3. What differences in cultural values were identified? Were the actions/behaviors of some group members helpful to you personally? To the group itself, in reaching consensus? Were there actions/behaviors that interfered with your group participation? If so, what were they?
4. What values do you hold that apply to this situation?
5. What did you learn?
6. How can you apply what you learned to your everyday life?

Debriefing Conclusions

1. Cultural values influence our beliefs about basic human nature, human relationships to nature, how we think about time, the balance between being and doing, and appropriate human relationships.
2. If our culture(s) have given us different values in any of these five areas, we may misunderstand and have conflicts with others.
3. Understanding our own values and those of others can help us reduce the misunderstandings and conflicts that can result from those differences.

Adapted from activities in *Developing Intercultural Awareness: A Cross-Cultural Training Handbook* by L. Robert Kohls and John M. Knight.

Cross-Cultural Values Worksheet

There are three statements following each number. Please choose one statement in each set that you *most agree* with and place a check next to that statement.

1._____ You must look out for yourself; most people cannot be trusted.

_____ There will always be people who will extend a helping hand to you, and there will also be those who will try to chop yours off.

_____ There's always someone who will lend a helping hand when you are in need because most people are basically good at heart.

2._____ Jails and prisons are necessary because people have an inclination toward evil.

_____ When children are young, they must be trained in the right ways. If they are left without guidance, they can go wrong just as easily as right.

_____ People are basically good and should be given the benefit of the doubt.

3._____ Life is largely determined by external forces, such as God or fate. A person cannot transcend the conditions that he or she is given.

_____ Humans should in every way live in complete harmony with nature.

_____ The human challenge is to conquer and control nature. Everything from skyscrapers to genetic engineering has resulted from our meeting this challenge.

4._____ Humans are only one creation of nature and must try to live in harmony with the others.

_____ Humans should never do anything to pollute the earth. "Mother Earth" is in charge and will ultimately win.

_____ Humans are nature's greatest accomplishment and their task is to control and perfect nature.

5._____ I look back with fondness on the days of my childhood. Those were the happiest days of my life, and most of what matters today started then.

_____ I live for the here and now because tomorrow is uncertain and yesterday is but a memory.

_____ You should plan ahead for the unexpected by putting aside a little money for a "rainy day."

6._____ We should learn from the past and emulate our ancestors.

_____ The present moment is everything. Make the most of it. Don't worry about tomorrow; enjoy today.

_____ Planning and goal setting make it possible to accomplish miracles. A little sacrifice today will bring a better tomorrow.

7._____ To love is better than to achieve; to be is better than to have.

_____ It is more important to pay attention to your inner development than to try to get ahead in life.

_____ Anything worth having is worth working for. Achievement is worth the effort it requires.

8._____ People's importance stems from their existence, not from the acts they perform.

_____ People's main purpose for being placed on earth is for their own inner development.

_____ If people work hard and apply themselves fully, their efforts will be rewarded.

9._____ Some people are born to lead and should be consulted when problems arise.

_____ Whenever a serious problem arises, family or close friends know best how to solve it.

_____ All people should have equal rights as well as complete control over their own destinies.

10._____ In times of difficulty, go to someone who has power to change the situation and ask for help.

_____ The most satisfying and effective form of decision making is group consensus.

_____ Any society that does not allow individuals to voice their dissent is not a free society.

Adapted from activities in *Developing Intercultural Awareness: A Cross-Cultural Training Handbook* by L. Robert Kohls and John M. Knight.

11

Contrasting Values

Adaptable

L

M

Time Required
70–85 minutes (20 minutes for small-group work; 20 minutes for large-group consensus process; 30–45 minutes for debriefing)

Objectives
1. To identify cultural values that are widely accepted in the United States
2. To contrast U.S. values with those held in other countries
3. To identify the implications of cultural differences when conducting business across national values differences

Materials
- Sets of "Contrasting Values" cards (run on cardstock paper or glue on index cards)
- Flipchart and tape
- Marking pens

Process
1. Prepare values cards by photocopying the "Contrasting Values" on card stock and cutting them into individual values cards. One complete set should be provided to each small group.
2. Place participants in groups of 3–5. Give each group a set of values cards, tape, and a flipchart page with "U.S. Values" printed on the left side and "Contrasting Values" printed on the right. Ask the group to tape each values card to the side of the easel page on which it belongs. Decisions should be based on the group's beliefs about dominant U.S. values.
3. In the large group, compare similarities and differences in the placement of each values card and try to reach consensus.
4. Discuss the potential implications of working or negotiating with people whose cultural values are not the same as U.S. values. Identify specific behavioral modifications that will increase effectiveness with groups who hold those contrasting values. *(Note: The trainer may wish to have a few examples to help the group get started, if necessary.)*

Debriefing Questions

1. For which values sets did you find it easiest to achieve agreement? Which were the hardest? Why?
2. How do you feel about the values that contrast with your own? Which values would be the most difficult for you to adapt to?
3. What personal values made these discussions challenging for you? What cultural values affected the discussion? Were there cultural values that made the discussion less difficult?
4. What have you learned?
5. How can you apply information from this experience to your everyday life?

Debriefing Conclusions

1. Identifying common U.S. cultural values can allow an individual to contrast her or his personal values with those of the larger culture.
2. Identifying contrasting cultural values can prepare us to be more effective working cross-culturally by adapting our behavior.
3. Identifying cultural values—both our own and those of others—can also help us to avoid stereotyping others (recognizing that there are individual differences within every culture) and to be more understanding when others may stereotype us.
4. Identifying the specific behaviors associated with values can also help us understand that the same value can be demonstrated in different behavioral ways.

Adapted from activities in *Developing Intercultural Awareness: A Cross-Cultural Training Handbook* by L. Robert Kohls and John M. Knight.

Contrasting Values

Rules Rigid	Rules Flexible
Change Positive	Tradition/Stability
Gender Equity	Male Superiority
Equality	Rank/Status/Hierarchy
Individualism	Group Welfare
Status Earned	Status Given
Competition Individual Achievement	Cooperation Group Achievement
Focus on Future	Focus on Present or Past
Action/Task-Oriented	People/Relationship-Oriented
Informality/ Casual Interaction	Formality/ Status Interaction
Directness	Indirectness
Direct Eye Contact	Eye Contact Avoided
Frankness/ "Honesty"	Harmony/Face Saving

Adapted from activities in *Developing Intercultural Awareness: A Cross-Cultural Training Handbook* by L. Robert Kohls and John M. Knight.

12

Origins of Cultural Contrasts

Time Required
45 minutes (15 minutes in pairs; 30 minutes for large-group discussion and debriefing)

Objectives
1. To identify some preferred values in the United States *(or the country in which the training is occurring)*
2. To explore the possible origins and basis for each value identified

Materials
- Cultural Contrast Statements Handout
- Value Contrasts Handout

Process
1. Provide each participant with a copy of the "Cultural Contrast Statements" and the "Value Contrasts" handouts and ask him or her to find a partner. Ask each pair to (a) identify which statement in each set is most reflective of U.S. American culture *(or any other national culture)*, (b) identify which value from the "Value Contrasts" handout its selected sentences might represent, and (c) speculate about what factors, historically, might have contributed to the formation of the identified value in U.S. American culture.
2. Bring the group back together and ask each pair to share one or more of its selected sentences, values, and ideas about the source of the value.

Debriefing Questions
1. Which statements or values were easier or more difficult to choose between? Why?
2. How easy was it to speculate about the origins of values? Why?
3. Were there differences between the contrasting statements that generated strong feelings in you or in your partner?
4. What values of yours might have affected your decision making?
5. What did you learn from this activity?
6. How can you apply information from this experience to your personal and/or work life?

Debriefing Conclusions

1. Understanding our own national cultural values can help us identify where our personal values agree with or differ from the national cultural norm.
2. Identifying the origin of cultural values can help us understand why we hold certain values.

Adapted from *Studying Abroad/Learning Abroad* by J. Daniel Hess.

Cultural Contrast Statements Handout

1. a. Age is to be respected.
    b. Young people understand the future.

2. a. It is important to discuss conflicts directly, the sooner the better.
    b. It is best to deal with conflict in a way that does not cause discomfort or embarrassment.

3. a. There is so much to be learned from the past. Following tradition gives us stability and a sense of direction.
    b. The world is moving at a faster and faster pace. Only those who can be flexible will be the leaders of tomorrow.

4. a. The true sign of an adult is the ability to stand up for oneself and be truly independent.
    b. It is important for family members to stick together and support each other.

5. a. The true meaning of being human lies in one's ability to develop spiritually. Without this, material wealth can be meaningless.
    b. Money is a symbol of success. If one is intelligent and willing to work hard, he or she will be able to satisfy most material desires.

6. a. We are all created equal. To treat someone as less than equal is violating that person's basic human rights.
    b. For society to have structure and order, it is important for each person to understand his or her "place."

7. a. It's important to speak up. How else will anyone know one's capabilities?
    b. Someone who boasts invites criticism, thus disrupting the social harmony.

8. a. When there's a question about something, it's best to ask rather than "beating around the bush."
    b. It's rude, insensitive, and just plain wrong to ask questions.

9. a. Calling someone "my friend" is presumptive and shows no respect for that person as an individual. How can such informality be trusted?
    b. It's important to get comfortable with each other before doing business. When the setting is too formal, the feeling is one of coldness and insincerity.

10. a. Show me the numbers. Get to the bottom line. Let's get right to the point so that we are all clear!
    b. Tell me the story. How did you come to this point? What are your feelings about the matter? What are other considerations?

Adapted from *Studying Abroad/Learning Abroad* by J. Daniel Hess.

Value Contrasts Handout

Equality	Hierarchy
Change	Tradition
Youth	Elders
Confrontation	Avoidance of Conflict
Informality	Formality
Materialism	Spirituality
Direct	Indirect
Boldness	Modesty
Independence	Dependence
Rational	Intuitive

Adapted from *Studying Abroad/Learning Abroad* by J. Daniel Hess.

Values of Performance Feedback

13

Work
L
P

Time Required

30 minutes

Objective

To prepare an individual to provide performance feedback to an employee in a way that most effectively matches the employee's and evaluator's values

Materials

• Values-Based Performance Feedback Form

Process

1. Complete the "Values-Based Performance Feedback" form.
2. In the column labeled "Employee Preference," place the letter (a) or (b) to indicate which of the two values in the "Values Continuum" column you believe the *employee* holds most strongly.
3. In the column labeled "Manager Preference," place the letter (a) or (b) to indicate which of the two values in the "Values Continuum" column *you* hold most strongly.
4. If the two columns match, no modification in preparation or presentation of feedback is likely to be required. If there are differences among some of the values pairs, however, you should consider how to present your feedback to best match the employee's value, thus increasing the successful understanding of the feedback. For example, if you value task and the employee values relationship, you will be most effective if you take time to establish or reestablish relationship with the employee before providing feedback. If, on the other hand, you value relationship and the employee values task, you will be most effective if you move directly into the feedback without taking time to chat.

Optional Process

If the organizational environment, or the employee, values two-way feedback, you may also want to ask the employee to complete this same form prior to delivering your feedback. This allows you to check your perception of the employee's values and may even offer an opportunity to discuss how value similarities/differences are affecting the manager/employee relationship.

Adapted from "Using Values-Based Performance Feedback to Motivate Employees" by Donna M. Stringer and Steve Guy in *Employment Relations Today*.

Values-Based Performance Feedback Form

Values Continuum	Feedback should focus on	Employee Preference	Manager Preference
Task/Relationship	a. specific measurable tasks b. relationships with co-workers and/or customers		
Individual/Team	a. individual achievement b. group performance		
Status, Hierarchy/ Equity	a. the manager giving feedback, which the employee receives without comment b. the employee and the manager providing feedback to each other		
Competition/ Cooperation	a. how the employee will benefit from good performance in comparison with other employees b. how the company benefits when all of the employees perform well		
Fate/Control	a. accepting what happens b. actively planning for the future; controlling my work life		
Locus of Control: Internal External	a. self-evaluation, which tells me how I am doing; others' feedback is relatively unimportant b. others' evaluations of me; this is how I best know how I am doing		

Adapted from "Using Values-Based Performance Feedback to Motivate Employees" by Donna M. Stringer and Steve Guy in *Employment Relations Today*.

14

What Do Others See?

Time Required

60 minutes (10 minutes for lecturette and instruction; 20 minutes for small-group discussions; 30 minutes for large-group debriefing and discussion)

Objectives

1. To explore interpretations of behavior from another cultural perspective
2. To discuss the values or beliefs that motivate the behavior
3. To identify behaviors that contribute to stereotypes of U.S. Americans

Materials

- What Do Others See? Handout
- Flipchart, pens, and tape

Process

1. Give a brief lecturette on the differences between stereotypes and generalizations (see Appendix E, page 241).
2. Place participants into groups of 4–6 people. Ask the group to read the "What Do Others See?" handout containing observations made by individuals from other cultures about U.S. Americans and then discuss the following questions for each observation:
   - Do you believe this to be a common stereotype of U.S. citizens?
   - Can you identify a U.S. value that might be motivating the behavior in the observation?
   - What value or values might influence the perception of someone from the culture being quoted about U.S. Americans?
   - What stereotype(s) might you hold of someone from these other nations based on these statements?
   - What specific behaviors might be helpful in encouraging greater cross-cultural understanding?
3. In the large group share the common stereotypes about U.S. citizens, identifying the U.S. American values that might lead to those stereotypes. Discuss any stereotypes identified for the other nations in the small groups and suggest behaviors for improving cross-cultural

understanding. Record the stereotypes (for the U.S. and for other nations) on one side of a flipchart and the values on the other side (for each observation) for the entire group to see. Use a second flipchart to record the behaviors identified for encouraging cross-cultural understanding.

Debriefing Questions

1. What happened? Where was it easiest for your small group to agree on stereotypes, values, or behaviors? Most difficult? Why?
2. How did you feel about the stereotypes (of the U.S. and those of the observers' countries) that the group identified? How do you feel about your group's reactions to the statements or stereotypes? How do you feel when you are stereotyped for any reason? When you find yourself stereotyping someone else?
3. What values affected the way you responded to this activity? What values did you hear spoken of or hinted at during the small-group discussion?
4. What did you learn?
5. How can you apply information from this experience to your everyday life?

Debriefing Conclusions

1. Cultural values influence our interpretation of behavior.
2. The broader a person's experience with a culture, the more accurate—and less stereotyped—his or her perceptions can be.
3. The behavior of someone from another culture is usually interpreted from the perspective of the interpreter's home cultural values.
4. Stereotypic statements are sometimes reinforced by the media.
5. Learning about the perceptions of someone from another culture may be helpful in understanding the impact of our actions.
6. Discussion of differences in perceptions can generate a wider variety of choices when we interact cross-culturally.

Optional Process

1. In small groups of 4–6 people, ask participants to develop a list of statements about their perceptions of people in one or more other countries that they have visited, lived in, or had contact with (known people from that country). After they have developed this list, ask them to write down the behaviors that led to those perceptions on one side of a sheet of newsprint, and the values the behaviors could represent on the other side.
2. In the large group, ask each small group to share the behaviors and values they have identified. Look for similarities or differences in perceptions of the same country across groups and discuss what might have led to any differences in perception. Examine the perceptions and decide which are stereotypes and which are valid generalizations.
3. Debrief using the same debriefing questions and conclusions.

Adapted from activities in *Developing Intercultural Awareness: A Cross-Cultural Training Handbook* by L. Robert Kohls and John M. Knight.

What Do Others See? Handout

Kenyan

"Americans appear to be rather distant. They are not really as close to other people—even fellow Americans—as Americans overseas portray.... It is like building a wall. Unless you ask an American a question, he will not even look at you. Individualism is very high."

Colombian

"The tendency in the U.S. to think that life is only work hits you in the face. Work seems to be the only motivation."

Indonesian

"I have been offended by how little Americans know about my country. They either think it is completely underdeveloped or that it is a jungle full of wild animals. Even when I find an American who knows something about Indonesia, it is only the negative things that he's heard about, such as our repressive government or the corruption of our officials."

Filipino

"They say children are the same. In my observations I found out a couple of ways where children differ. Children in the United States are very forward in their way of speaking, even to their parents and elders. They show a lack of respect for age. Also, I have observed that children in the U.S. don't offer their services to their parents willingly. They either have to be told what is to be done or they have to be given some reward or compensation for what they do."

Somalian

"I am worried that you have too much democracy in America. There are so many separate voices and so many selfish interests that you cannot accomplish anything for the general good of the country. You are even prevented from controlling your criminal element for fear of denying the criminal his rights. That's too much freedom for your own good."

Iranian

"It is puzzling when Americans apply the word *friend* to acquaintances from almost every sector of their past or present life, without necessarily implying close ties or inseparable bonds."

Taiwanese

"Before I came to America, I always heard how hardworking Americans are, but compared to my people, they don't seem to work very hard at all. Why, Americans only work five days a week."

Swedish

"I have been most negatively impressed by the patronizing attitude of many Americans with whom I discussed Third-World countries. Some of them were very definite in saying they believed that the people in the Third World were underdeveloped because they were lazy and did not work hard enough."

Japanese

"Family life in the United States seems harsh and unfeeling compared to the close ties in our country. Americans do not seem to care for their elderly parents."

Korean

"In a twelfth-grade social studies class, the teacher gave choices of assignment for the next class. I didn't like the idea of pupils choosing the assignment. I wonder what these pupils will do later in life when there are no choices in the duty assigned to them. They must learn while they are in school how to do well the jobs assigned to them from above."

Sudanese

"The hardest thing for me to accept and get used to when I first came to your country was how impersonal everything was. Whenever I bought a Coca-Cola or a chocolate bar or a postage stamp I had to buy it from a machine rather than from a living person. You can't talk to a machine and even when it gives you a candy bar, it cannot establish a satisfying relationship with you. But in your country many people want to spend time by themselves rather than talking to other people in a friendly conversation."

Indian

"Americans seem to be in a perpetual hurry. Just watch the way they walk down the street. They never allow themselves the leisure of enjoying life; there are too many things to do."

Algerian

"I was horrified at the ignorance of the high school students about my country—Algeria. They knew nothing at all about it—location, people, language, political condition. What made it even worse was the ignorance of the teacher herself. Her knowledge was very shallow and, in certain instances, quite erroneous."

Colombian

"I was surprised, in the United States, to find so many young people were not living with their parents, although they were not married. Also, I was surprised to see so many single people of all ages living alone, eating alone, and walking the streets alone. The U.S. must be the loneliest country in the world."

Indonesian

"The questions Americans ask me are sometimes very embarrassing, like whether I have ever seen a camera. Most of them consider themselves the most highly civilized people. Why? Because they are accustomed to technical inventions? Consequently, they think that people living in bamboo houses or having different customs from theirs are primitive and backward."

Adapted from an activity in *Developing Intercultural Awareness: A Cross-Cultural Training Handbook* by L. Robert Kohls and John M. Knight.

15

Five Values

Time Required

60–75 minutes (30 minutes to play, 10–15 minutes to report results, 20–30 for debriefing)

Objectives

1. To explore the behavioral applications of five important team values
2. To practice turning invisible values into observable behaviors
3. To brainstorm ideas on values as related to teamwork, the organization, or the customer.

Materials

- Five value envelopes
- Five index cards for each team
- Flipchart and tape
- A whistle and a timer
- Prize (if Optional Process 1 is used)

Process

1. Organize the participants into five teams. Briefly identify the five values the teams will be discussing; for example, trust, diversity, customer service, quality, integrity, or any five values that are relevant to this group of participants. *(Note: If you are working with an organization or team that has written core values, select five of their written values to enhance the relevance.)*
2. Give each team an envelope that has one of the five values written on the outside. Inside you will have placed five blank index cards.
3. Round 1: Each team discusses the value shown on their envelope. Give them three minutes to discuss specific behaviors in their workplace that exemplify the value on their envelope. Ask them to generate as many behaviors as possible during the time allotted and to list those behaviors on one of the index cards. At the end of the round, teams will place their index cards into the value envelope and pass the envelope to the next group.
4. Rounds 2–5: Repeat the same process. Each time, the teams discuss

the value on the envelope and list specific behaviors that demonstrate the value on a blank index card. They should not look at the applications suggested by other teams.

5. Round 6: Now give the teams their original envelopes. Ask them to combine all of the ideas on the cards and record them on a piece of newsprint to be posted and reported to the entire group. Allow approximately 10 minutes for this process.

6. Each team reports to the group the behaviors that have been identified as demonstrating the value they have been assigned.

Debriefing Questions:

1. What happened as you identified behaviors that demonstrated each value? Which values were easiest to identify behaviors for? Hardest? Why?
2. How did you feel about the process?
3. What differences emerged in the group as you described behaviors that demonstrate certain values?
4. What did you learn?
5. How can you apply this learning to your everyday work?

Debriefing Conclusions

1. We often assume we know what a specific behavior means, or how to express a certain value.
2. Individuals may see the same value in different behaviors or different values in the same behavior.
3. We tend to jump to conclusions (often unconsciously) about what value is being expressed by a behavior.
4. The more behaviorally specific we can be in our expectations, the more likely people are to meet those expectations. Broad value expectations can lead to misinterpretations, judgments, and conflict.
5. Organization or team expectations are not often examined to determine how they affect employee diversity or inclusion.

Optional Processes

Option 1—A Competitive Approach. During Round 6, ask teams to evaluate the behaviors on the five cards in their envelope and to distribute a total of 100 points among the five cards. Allow approximately 10 minutes. Check with teams at the end of the 10 minutes to be sure they have had adequate time to evaluate the responses.

Each team will report the value written on their envelope and then share the behaviors written on each index card. The cards should be read from lowest- to highest-scoring cards. After reading the five cards, the team should announce the points that each received and the criteria used to determine the points.

All of the cards should be placed on a table in a line under the "value envelope." A representative from each team should come to collect the cards from her or his team. Teams then total the points on their cards and announce their points. The highest-scoring team wins the prize.

Option 2—Organizational Implications (following Round 6). After the whole group has time to examine the behaviors listed, ask if any of the listed behaviors might get in the way of valuing diversity, or of being inclusive in an organization. Lead a discussion on issues raised by the group.

Ask if those behaviors that are identified are necessary to conducting the organization's business in a safe, legal, productive, and cost-effective manner. If they are not, ask how the team or organization might modify their behavioral expectations. If the behaviors are necessary, ask how the team or organization can communicate the necessity for this behavioral expectation in a way that is respectful of employee differences.

Adapted from an activity presented by Sivasailam Thiagarajan at The Summer Institute for Intercultural Communication, 2000.

16

What Would You Say?

Work

L–M

P, T

Time Required

60 minutes (5 minutes to complete worksheet; 20 minutes in groups; 20 minutes for group reports; 15 minutes for debriefing)

Objectives

1. To encourage participants to identify their own stereotypes and prejudices
2. To stimulate discussion of issues that are often avoided (the "undiscussables")
3. To provide practice in tactfully dealing with prejudices when they are encountered

Materials

- What Would You Say? Worksheet

Process

1. Ask each participant to complete the "What Would You Say?" worksheet by writing *A* (agree) or *D* (disagree) by each of the statements.
2. Place participants in groups of 3–5 people.
3. Ask the groups to discuss each statement and try to reach a consensus about it. If all of the group members cannot come to an agreement on a statement, they will rewrite the statement in such a way that all group members can agree. *(Note: Be clear that agreeing to disagree is not a solution. It is just a way of avoiding the activity.)*
4. Ask the teams to come together as a group and share the statements they have revised, including the process they used to come to agreement.

Debriefing Questions

1. What happened? Which statements were the most difficult to reach consensus on? Why?
2. How did you feel during the process?
3. What values may have been affecting either the group discussion or your own feelings about the process?
4. What have you learned?

5. How will you apply what you have learned to your everyday work life?

Debriefing Conclusions

1. Our own values affect the way we perceive statements and how we participate in conversations where people disagree.
2. Listening to others' opinions often leads to greater understanding.
3. If our goal is to come to consensus, we can almost always find a way if we are committed to doing so.

Adapted from an activity designed by L. Robert Kohls in *Intercultural Sourcebook: Cross-Cultural Training Methods*, vol. 2, edited by Sandra M. Fowler and Monica G. Mumford.

What Would You Say? Worksheet

Please read each of the following statements. Write *A* next to the statements that you agree with and *D* next to statements that you disagree with. You will be asked to share your responses with others during the next part of this activity.

_____ People who use all of their sick leave or vacation don't care about the business.

_____ Immigrants and foreign nationals should speak English when they are in U.S. workplaces.

_____ Good managers spend time providing feedback (both positive and corrective) to their employees.

_____ The most effective teams get to know each other before jumping into their task.

_____ Being loud and gregarious in the workplace is inappropriate.

_____ People who want to resolve issues all the time create conflict in the workplace.

_____ Being a "take charge" person is a characteristic of all good leaders.

_____ The most important qualities to exhibit if you plan to develop a trusting business relationship are being straightforward and direct.

_____ People who are late with assignments or meetings don't care about the team (or the organization).

_____ People who come to work sick are dedicated employees.

_____ People who don't contribute to group discussions are not good team members.

_____ People who prefer to work individually rarely contribute to teams.

_____ People who resist change don't belong in today's workplace.

_____ People who are organized and systematic about everything miss opportunities to be creative.

_____ People who rely on the organizational hierarchy rather than making their own decisions are too fearful to be creative.

Adapted from an activity designed by L. Robert Kohls in *Intercultural Sourcebook: Cross-Cultural Training Methods*, vol. 2, edited by Sandra M. Fowler and Monica G. Mumford.

17

Generational Values

Time Required

75–90 minutes (15 minutes for individual work; 30 minutes for small-group discussion; 30–45 minutes for large-group reports and debriefing)

Objectives

1. To identify how age affects values, behaviors, and cross-age perceptions
2. To identify how perceptions and conflict in any work team may be affected by age-related values

Materials

- Important Events for Age Cohorts Handout
- Core Values of Each Age Cohort Handout
- How Each Cohort Sees the World Handout

Background Material for Instructors

- Motivating Each Age Cohort

Process

1. Provide each participant with the handouts "Important Events for Age Cohorts," "Core Values of Each Age Cohort," and "How Each Cohort Sees the World." Give participants 10–15 minutes to read and digest the material.

   Note: If you have an opportunity to do so, give people the handouts the day before the activity so the reflective learners will have time to fully process the information. Caution people that this information should not be used to stereotype others based on their age. There are always individuals within each age group who do not match the profile. Nonetheless, in large groups, these descriptors can be helpful.

2. Place participants in small groups of 4–6 people. Ask them to imagine that they have a work team that includes people from each of the four age cohorts (veterans, boomers, gen Xers, nexters). Then instruct them to answer the following questions as a group:

- What strength could each cohort bring to your team?
- What strategy or strategies could you use to maximize those strengths?
- What conflicts might occur across cohorts on the team?
- What strategy could you use to minimize potential conflicts?

Note: If you feel the group needs assistance, suggest that they consider a specific situation, such as budgets, replacement of old equipment, job security, voluntary overtime, or other work-related situations specific to the organization in which the participants are working.

3. Ask each small group to report one strength and one conflict to the larger group, including the strategies identified to maximize the strength and minimize the conflict.

Debriefing Questions

1. What happened during your small-group discussions? What (strength or conflict) was easiest to identify? What was hardest? Why?
2. How did you feel during the small-group discussion? Were there ideas or discussion items you were either more or less comfortable with? Why? Were there cohort values that emerged even during this small-group discussion?
3. How closely do your personal values match those of your cohort group?
4. What have you learned?
5. How can you apply what you have learned to teamwork in your workplace setting?

Debriefing Conclusions

1. As one ages, he or she accumulates life experiences; these in turn result in changing values. Those value differences can lead to different behaviors at work and can benefit work teams. They can also create misperceptions and conflict.
2. Individuals may blend the values of their own age cohort with those of their parents'. Individual experience will also determine the degree to which a person's values match those of his or her cohort.
3. Identifying what someone values will enable us to work more effectively with that person and to understand how to motivate him or her more effectively.

Optional Debriefing Questions (for use in training managers):

1. How would you motivate people from each cohort group?
2. How would you treat age cohorts differently if you were recruiting for new employees?
3. How would you mentor someone from each age cohort?
4. Based on your age cohort and your core values, which age cohort may be most difficult for you to work with? Why? What strategies might you engage in to reduce your discomfort and improve your effectiveness?

© Executive Diversity Services, Inc., Seattle, Washington, 1997.

Important Events for Age Cohorts Handout

Veterans	Boomers	Gen Xers
1927—Lindbergh completes first transatlantic flight	1954—McCarthy HCUAA hearings being conducted	1970—Women's liberation protests and demonstrations
1929—Stock market crashes	1955—Salk vaccine tested on the public	1972—Arab terrorists at Munich Olympics
1930—U.S. Depression deepens	1955—Rosa Parks refuses to move to the back of the bus in Montgomery, Alabama	1973—Watergate scandal; energy crisis begins
1931—"Star-Spangled Banner" becomes national anthem	1957—First nuclear power plant; Congress passes the Civil Rights Act	1976—Tandy and Apple market PCs
1932—FDR elected	1960—Birth control pills introduced; John F. Kennedy elected	1978—Mass suicide in Jonestown
1933—The Dust Bowl; The New Deal	1961—Kennedy establishes Peace Corps	1979—Three Mile Island nuclear reactor nears meltdown; U.S. corporations begin massive layoffs; Iran holds sixty-six Americans hostage
1934—Social Security system established	1962—Cuban Missile Crisis; John Glenn circles the earth	1980—John Lennon shot and killed
1937—Hitler invades Austria	1963—Marin Luther King Jr. leads march on Washington, D.C.; President Kennedy assassinated	1980—Ronald Reagan inaugurated
1940—U.S. prepares for war	1965—U.S. sends ground combat troops to Vietnam	1986—Challenger disaster
1941—Pearl Harbor; U.S. enters World War II	1966—National Organization for Women founded; Cultural Revolution in China	1987—Stock market plummets
1944—D day in Normandy	1967—American Indian Movement founded	1988—Terrorist bomb blows up Pan Am flight 103 over Lockerbie, Scotland
1945—Victory in Europe and Japan	1968—Martin Luther King Jr. and Robert F. Kennedy assassinated	1989—*Exxon Valdez* oil tanker spill; Fall of Berlin Wall; Tienanmen Square
1950—Korean War	1969—First lunar landing; Woodstock	1990—Nelson Mandela released from prison

Veterans	Boomers	Gen Xers
Golden days of radio Silver screen Labor unions	1970—Kent State University shootings	1991—Operation Desert Storm
	Television Suburbia	1992—Rodney King beating videotaped, Los Angeles riots
		MTV AIDS Single-parent homes

Core Values of Each Age Cohort Handout

Veterans	Boomers	Gen Xers	Nexters
Adherence to rules	Affiliation/Relationships	Adventure	Achievement
Civic pride	Importance of heart and humanity in the workplace	Balance	Civic duty
Conformity	Calmness; unflappable under duress	Casualness toward authority	Confidence
Conservatism	Fairness; civil rights	Diversity	Diversity
Consistency and uniformity	Health and wellness	Fun	Manners
Dedication and sacrifice	Individualism	Informality	Morality
Delayed reward	Instant gratification	Nontraditional orientation toward time and space	Optimism
Dependability	Involvement	Pragmatism	Sociability
Discipline	Optimism	Self-reliance	Nonviolence
Duty before pleasure	Participation and inclusion	Sense of family through friends	Street smarts
Hard work	Personal freedom	Global thinking	Tolerance
Honor	Personal gratification	Skepticism	
Law and order	Personal growth	Technoliteracy	
Preference for things on a grand scale	Social justice		
Logic	Stars of the show Center of attention		
Loyalty	Teamwork oriented		
Obedience	Youth		
Past oriented/history			
Patience			
Persistence			
Respect for authority			
Save and pay cash			

How Each Cohort Sees the World Handout

	Veterans	Boomers	Gen Xers	Nexters
Outlook	Practical	Optimistic	Skeptical	Hopeful
Media impact	Radio	Television	Computer	Internet
Work ethic	Dedicated	Driven	Balanced	Determined
View of authority	Respectful	Love/hate	Unimpressed	Polite
Leadership by	Hierarchy	Consensus	Competence	Pulling together
Relationships	Personal sacrifice	Personal gratification	Reluctance to commit	Inclusive
Turnoffs	Vulgarity	Political incorrectness	Cliché, hype	Promiscuity

Adapted from *Generations at Work: Managing the Clash of Veterans, Boomers, Xers, and Nexters*, copyright (C) 2000, Performance Research Associates, Inc., Ron Zemke, Claire Raines, Bob Filipczak. AMACOM, a division of American Managment Association, New York, NY. Used by permission of the publisher. All rights reserved.

Motivating Each Age Cohort

Veterans
- Acknowledge their experience. Demonstrate that you value it by asking them to contribute ideas or skills.
- Ask them to tell you what has or has not worked in the past.
- Acknowledge their perseverance and length of service.
- Refer to the workplace as a family.
- Appeal to loyalty.
- Be consistent.

Boomers
- Tell them how you expect them to contribute to your success.
- Publicly acknowledge their contributions and successes.
- Notice—and acknowledge—any unique contributions they make.
- Tell them you need them—and tell them why.
- Give them approval as often as possible.
- Create a participatory, fair, casual work environment.
- Get to know them personally.
- Let them be in charge of something and dabble in several things.

Gen Xers
- Give them the end goal desired and let them achieve it in their own way.
- Provide them with the newest technology.
- Keep rules to a minimum.
- Create a workplace that is as informal as possible, with very little hierarchy.
- Tell them why they are doing things—they want reasons.
- Spend time with them—they appreciate relationships.
- Mentor them early in their tenure so they can succeed.
- Help them know what is expected. They want specific responsibilities, goals, standards, opportunities, and rewards.
- Encourage them to find creative ways to have fun while getting the job done.

Nexters
- Tell them how bright and creative others in the workplace are.
- Give them a boss who is in her or his sixties.
- Tell them you expect them and their co-workers to turn the company around.
- Tell them you expect them to be heroes.

Adapted from *Generations at Work: Managing the Clash of Veterans, Boomers, Xers, and Nexters,* copyright (C) 2000, Performance Research Associates, Inc., Ron Zemke, Claire Raines, Bob Filipczak. AMACOM, a division of American Managment Association, New York, NY. Used by permission of the publisher. All rights reserved.

18

Team Values Assessment

```
Work

L–M

P, T, D
```

Time Required
60 minutes (10 minutes for individual work; 45 minutes for discussion; 5 minutes to summarize debriefing conclusions)

Objectives
1. To provide a team with an opportunity to identify similar and different values
2. To facilitate a team's identification of its strengths and challenges based on a values profile

Materials
- Flipchart
- Sticky dots
- Team Values Assessment Worksheet

Process
1. Distribute the "Team Values Assessment" worksheet and ask the participants to complete it.
2. On a flipchart, write the following, allowing plenty of space for participants to place their sticky dots under the numbers.

Harmony	1 2 3 4 5	Surfacing and resolving differences
Group performance	1 2 3 4 5	Individual performance
Internal control	1 2 3 4 5	External control
Task/product	1 2 3 4 5	Relationship/process
Change	1 2 3 4 5	Tradition

3. Give each person five sticky dots. Ask participants to place one under the number on each line that corresponds to their answers on the worksheet, spreading the dots out so they can be tallied.
4. Based on the placement of the dots, ask the team to identify the challenges they might face in working together.
5. Ask the team to identify strategies for maximizing their strengths and reducing the challenges they have identified. Encourage them to agree on specific behaviors they will use or avoid in carrying out these strategies.

Note: The dots clustered in one location could be a strength but could also be a weakness because the team is missing another value perspective. If the dots are polarized, this could be a source of internal team conflict.

Debriefing Conclusions

1. Individuals bring their personal values to teams. Similar values across the team can be a strength (source of compatibility) or a weakness (lacking the perspective of the different value).
2. Inconsistent values among team members may be a source of conflict.
3. Sources of conflict can be reduced when a team is willing to openly discuss values and to identify ways to manage the differences.

Team Values Assessment Worksheet

Please circle the answer that is closest to your point of view in each of the five areas.

A. Harmony or Surfacing and Resolving Differences
 1. Disagreement is to be avoided at all costs.
 2. Maintaining harmony is the primary value; anything can be worked out through the informal network without verbal conflict or embarrassment.
 3. I don't like conflict, but I am willing to engage in it when it is necessary to get the job done.
 4. Conflict can be creative and productive, but it should be well managed.
 5. Disagreements must be aired; harmony is secondary and is restored through direct verbal resolution.

B. Group or Individual Performance
 1. I strongly prefer working in groups, and I am always careful to include people who need to be there or who may feel that they are being left out.
 2. I like group work because of the broad range of input it brings to the issues.
 3. I think sometimes group work is useful, depending on the task.
 4. We can spend too much time in groups, losing focus and clouding the issues.
 5. Groups are time wasters; I'd far rather work alone.

C. Internal or External Control
 1. Fate is in our hands; we can identify and solve any problem with the assistance of analytical techniques and formalized problem-solving skills.
 2. I can usually have an effect on my environment.
 3. About half the time I have control over a situation, and half the time I just have to live with it.
 4. The plan is pretty well set, but I can control how I respond to it.
 5. Most issues are resolved by someone more senior than I; my job is to make the best of the plan.

D. Task/Product or Relationship/Process
 1. We're here to do a job. If we are to be competitive, we have to focus on the task.
 2. We try to move quickly and get the job done, even if we also have to work with people we don't much care for.
 3. How we interact with other team members has an impact on the product; I try to consider both.
 4. We can't do anything without people; the best decision must first take people into consideration.
 5. It isn't what we do but how we do it that counts. The best decision is useless if the process has been bad; it won't work.

E. Change or Tradition
 1. If something isn't broken, don't fix it.
 2. If something isn't working, we should fix it but only after we are really sure it won't work.
 3. If something is broken, it will take care of itself. All things seek balance if we don't tinker with them.
 4. Change is usually creative and good; the status quo makes us lazy thinkers.
 5. Change is almost always productive. It generates fresh ideas, products, and programs.

19

International Cultural Values

Time Required

75–120 minutes (30 minutes for small-group discussion; 45–90 minutes for discussion and debriefing, depending on the number of cultural groups)

> *Note: This activity requires that there be multiple identifiable cultural groups in the training, representing national differences, ethnic or racial differences, occupational differences, or gender differences. The instructions are written for national differences. You can readily modify the instructions for use with other group differences.*

Objectives

1. To identify culture-specific values of the participants
2. To identify how these values affect behavior in the workplace
3. To examine cross-cultural workplace perceptions
4. To identify effective cross-cultural workplace adaptations

Materials

- Flipchart and marking pens
- Masking tape to post the newsprint
- Differences in Cultural Values Worksheet (see Appendix B, page 233)
- Values Differences Handout (see Appendix C, page 235)

Process

1. Give each participant a copy of the "Differences in Cultural Values" worksheet (Appendix B) and the "Values Differences" handout (Appendix C). Ask participants to group themselves by their country of origin.
2. Ask each group to identify and circle the primary value of their country of origin on each row of the "Differences in Cultural Values" worksheet. Tell them they can refer to the "Values Differences" handout for more information, should they need it. Ask them to describe how these values would be demonstrated behaviorally in the workplace, using newsprint to do so. Give them approximately 30 minutes for this discussion.

3. Ask each group to display their descriptions and to report their values and behaviors to the large group.
4. In the large group, discuss the following:
   - Where are there differences in values? Behaviors?
   - How might these differences be misinterpreted in the workplace?
   - What tools or behaviors could help reduce misperceptions?

Debriefing Questions

1. What happened during your culture-specific discussion?
2. How did you feel during the culture-specific discussion? As you listened to other groups reporting?
3. What personal values do you hold that are different from those of your country of origin? What values do you hold that have been challenged during this activity?
4. What have you learned?
5. How can you apply what you learned to your workplace?

Debriefing Conclusions

1. Although culture-specific values and behaviors may be identifiable, there are also individual differences within any cultural group.
2. When individuals from two or more countries work together, they may contribute different culturally based work values. The differences in values can offer additional resources. They may also result in misperceptions and conflict.
3. Understanding the differences in cultural values can help us avoid conflict and enable us to discuss conflicts when they occur.

20

Work Values

> **Work**
>
> **L–M**
>
> **P, T, D, M**

Time Required

60 minutes (30 minutes for small-group work; 10 minutes for group reports; 20 minutes for debriefing)

Objectives

1. To encourage people to think and talk about their own values and life histories as related to work, including culturally embodied patterns
2. To explore possible team conflicts that occur when an individual's values are not consistent with the group values
3. To explore possible conflicts that can occur between individuals based on value differences

Materials

- Flipchart and marking pens
- Masking tape to hang paper on walls

Process

Note: This activity will get off to a good start if you begin with a story from your personal life to demonstrate what is expected and to help participants feel some safety in the request to share personal information.

1. Divide participants into small groups of 4–7 and give them approximately 30 minutes to discuss the following questions:
   - What messages or lessons did you learn from your family about work? Who taught you? How?
   - At what age did you first start paid employment? Describe what you did.
   - What was positive about this first work experience?
   - What work-related values do you hold today based on any of the above?
2. Ask each group to write on newsprint the values identified, potential value conflicts within the group, and strategies or behaviors that could help the group avoid or resolve value differences.
3. Ask a representative from each small group to report on one potential value issue and the group's suggestions for ways to avoid or resolve the conflict.

Debriefing Questions

1. What happened during your group discussions? What similarities or differences did you identify in childhood messages?
2. How did you feel during the small-group discussion? Were there people whose values you identified with? Didn't feel comfortable with? Why?
3. What personal values were touched on during your discussion? Did any of your values make this discussion easier or more difficult?
4. What have you learned? What potential conflicts did you identify?
5. How can you use what you learned in your everyday work life? What specific tools or strategies were you able to identify to avoid or reduce conflicts?

Debriefing Conclusions

1. Early lessons from our family and our earliest work experiences help to shape our work values.
2. We each bring our values to work. When our values differ from the values of others at work, conflicts may result.
3. A group has the ability to identify ways to avoid or reduce value-based conflicts. The most important step is a willingness to discuss the differences in nonjudgmental ways.

Adapted from an activity by Carol Wolf in *Experiential Activities for Intercultural Learning*, edited by H. Ned Seelye.

21

In My Family

Time Required

60 minutes (30 minutes for small-group discussion; 30 minutes for large-group discussion and debriefing)

Objectives

1. To identify how the value of respect was defined behaviorally in each participant's family
2. To identify how the differences in definitions may lead to different behaviors at work and result in possible misunderstandings

Materials

- Flipchart and marking pens

Process

1. Assign participants to small groups of 3–5 people and give the groups approximately 30 minutes to discuss the following:
   - When I was growing up, who got respect in my family and elsewhere? Why?
   - How, specifically, did I treat that (those) individual(s) to demonstrate my respect? (Ask participants to focus on roles such as "parent," not the names of specific individuals.)
2. While the small groups hold their discussions, write the headings "Who," "Why," and "Behaviors" across the top of a sheet of newsprint.
3. Ask each small group to report the results of its discussion. As each group reports, record on the newsprint under the three columns who got respect and why and the specific behaviors identified, for example,

Who	Why	Behaviors
Parents	Authority, age, experience	Obeyed, didn't challenge
Teachers	Authority, knowledge, age	Obeyed, didn't challenge, questioned to learn
Police officers	Authority, power (guns)	Obeyed, asked for help, feared/avoided

4. Select some contrasts and ask participants to discuss implications that this might have for the workplace.

As an example from the above chart, someone might say that a teacher received respect "just because" (status given). Someone else might say the teacher got respect because he or she worked hard to get an education (status earned). These different values regarding the granting of status might be exhibited in workplace behavior toward supervisors and managers. Conflict could occur if the supervisor learned that given status (i.e., the status given to the supervisor upon promotion to that position) was the key to respect and if the employee learned that status (i.e., respect) is earned by demonstrating one's skills. The employee might not be displaying the respect that the supervisor feels she deserves.

Another example might be that many people get respect just because they are older. Explore the implications of this if the supervisor is younger than someone he or she supervises. Might this lead the supervisor to be somewhat reluctant to assert authority? Might this lead the employee to be more reluctant to listen to and take direction from the supervisor?

Ask the group to give other examples of potential value conflicts from the lists.

Note: This activity requires that you, as the facilitator, understand cultural value systems and have the ability to listen carefully for those values, because the participants may not know the reasons why they respect someone or the values that underlie their behaviors or expectations.

Debriefing Questions

1. What happened? Where were there similarities? Differences?
2. How did you feel during these discussions? Were you alone in your choices? Was it easy or difficult to identify the reasons and/or behaviors? Why?
3. What values do you hold as an individual that were challenged during the discussion? Are there organizational values that are difficult for you because of your personal values?
4. What have you learned about yourself? About others?
5. How can you apply what you have learned to the workplace?

Debriefing Conclusions

1. We learn values very early from our families—and later, from others—including who gets respect and why.
2. We learn how to behave in order to show respect very early—and those behaviors may not be the same for everyone.
3. Early lessons about who gets respect and how we should show it can affect the way we act and perceive others' actions in the work environment.
4. If we have different ways of showing respect, it can lead to misperceptions and potential conflict.

22

Group Commandments

Time Required

60 minutes (5 minutes for individual work; 15 minutes for small-group work; 20 minutes for large-group discussion; 20 minutes for debriefing)

Objectives

1. To assist participants in identifying how their values affect their unwritten rules for others
2. To make explicit values that may be implicit
3. To identify the ways these rules can create "insiders" and "outsiders"

Materials

- Paper and pencils or pens
- Flipchart and marking pens
- Masking tape for posting small-group results

Process

1. Introduction: Every group and organization has a set of rules or "commandments" that help regulate activity within the group or organization. Give the following instructions to the group: There are similar "shoulds" and "should nots" that each of us carries around (often unconsciously) by which we evaluate others. I'd like you to take the next five minutes to write down four or five commandments that you personally feel a member of any work group should follow.

   Note: You may wish to give a few examples from your own valued "commandments" to get the group started.

2. Place participants in groups of 3–5 and ask them to share their commandments, identifying any that they have in common. Each group should identify *three* that they want to share with the larger group and list these on easel pages.

3. Ask all of the small groups to share their lists with the large group and to look for similarities and differences. Beginning with the most common "rules," ask if it might be possible for someone to violate any of these rules without knowing it. Are there any individuals or

groups that might feel like outsiders because of this commandment? How might the commandment be modified to be more inclusive?

Example: "Group members must not leave early—they owe the company a full day's work." This commandment could be a disadvantage for an employee who has day-care issues (either children or elderly). These people may be taking work home or coming in early to give the company a full day's work. Modification could be "Group members give the company a full day's work for a full day's pay."

Debriefing Questions

1. Did you have any trouble identifying four or five commandments?
2. How easy was it to come to consensus in the small group regarding the three most important rules to share?
3. How did you feel during the discussions? Were there voices that did not get heard? How inclusive was the discussion; that is, did any individual(s) dominate the conversation?
4. What personal or organizational values were challenged during the discussions? How did that happen?
5. How can you apply what you have learned to your everyday work life?

Debriefing Conclusions

1. Our values often translate into unconscious commandments to which we hold ourselves and others.
2. When those commandments are unwritten, the values and assumptions that they are based on cannot be examined.
3. When those unwritten rules become overt, they can be discussed and made more inclusive, based on group or individual needs.

23

I Am

Time Required

60 minutes (15 minutes for individual work; 15 minutes for small-group discussion; 30 minutes for debriefing)

Objectives

1. To identify personal values
2. To encourage discussion of individual values as a team-building activity
3. To identify the impact of consistency/inconsistency in personal and organizational or team values

Materials

- Paper and pencil to record responses

Process

1. Ask each participant to write 20 descriptive statements that begin with "I am...".
2. Ask each participant to identify the 10 descriptors that are most important to him or her. Now ask each one to choose the 5 most important statements.

   Note: What you are doing is asking people to make value judgments regarding what is most important to them about themselves. Be prepared for some groans.

3. Place participants in small groups of 3–5 and ask them to share their top 5 statements, looking for areas of similarity and difference. Tell them to then discuss what values they hold that are represented in their top 5 statements.
4. Ask participants to return to the larger group for debriefing.

Debriefing Questions

1. Describe what happened. What made it easy or difficult to write 20 "I am..." statements? What made it easy or difficult to reduce those to the most important 10, then to 5?
2. How did you feel about sharing your list with others? How did you feel when you identified similarities or differences with others?

3. What personal, organizational, or national cultural values came into play in your initial list? The reduced lists? Are there organizational values that are a particularly good or poor match with your personal values? How might that match, or lack thereof, affect your work in the organization?
4. What have you learned about yourself? About others? About the organization?
5. How could you apply information from this experience to real life? How might the information be used to improve teamwork? Job satisfaction? Productivity? Organizational and/or career planning?

Debriefing Conclusions

1. Adjectives and traits that we use to describe ourselves reflect our values and beliefs.
2. Values differences can affect individual, team, and organizational effectiveness.
3. Identifying values similarities can improve teamwork and relationship development.
4. Understanding values differences can facilitate effective working relationships.
5. Job satisfaction occurs most often when individual and organizational values are aligned.

Alternate Process

This activity can be used as an icebreaker in a training session or as a way to begin a team-building session with an already existing work team. When you start the large-group debriefing, have all of the participants introduce themselves or another member of their small group, using one of their top 5 "I am..." statements.

Adapted from research described by Harry C. Triandis for *Culture and Social Behavior*, published in 1994 by McGraw-Hill.

24

U.S. American Values

Time Required

60 minutes (30 minutes for small-group work; 30 minutes for large-group discussion and debriefing)

Objectives

1. To identify U.S. American values
2. To identify individual differences within the same culture
3. To explore ways that cultural values influence our perceptions of those from other cultural backgrounds
4. To discuss how and why values differ from culture to culture
5. To discuss the possible consequences of judging the values held by those from another culture based on our own cultural perspective

Materials

- A U.S. American Values Handout for each group
- A set of 16 blank index cards for each group

Process

1. Reproduce the "U.S. American Values" handout on card-stock paper.
2. Place participants in groups of 3–4 and provide each group with one copy of the handout and a set of 16 index cards. Ask each group to write down all of the values from the handout, one per index card. Then instruct each group to read over the set of values cards and try to reach consensus on a rank ordering for the cards, based on what they believe to be the most highly valued U.S. cultural values (not personal values). Some groups may disagree with the values listed or wish to add other values to the list. Ask groups to keep track of the values they would like to remove or add to the list—so that they can share these values (and their rationale) with the larger group when they reconvene—but not to include the additinal values on the prioritized listing. Use these removed or added values as an additional learning opportunity.
3. Ask the small groups to reconvene in the larger group, share their rankings, and identify the rationale they used to prioritize their values lists. If most or all of the small groups were able to agree on

the values priorities, ask the large group to try to reach consensus on a final prioritization. If, however, the small groups disagree with each other's priorities and can identify solid reasons for doing so, allow the differences to remain, pointing out that our experiences can lead to different priorities and that such an experience should be used to learn about differences rather than demanding that there be "one right answer."

4. Ask participants to identify a culture where each of these 16 values may not be considered important. Explore influences (historical, geographical, political, economic) that may have had an effect on the values in that culture.

   Note: Even if all of the facts are not available, the activity stimulates thinking about the cultural relativity of values. The trainer may want to be prepared to give one or two examples.

Debriefing Questions

1. What happened (a) as your group began to sort the values, (b) as you identified values that were not included or that you wanted to add or eliminate, and (c) as your group discussed cultural factors that influence values?
2. How did you feel about the values chosen for the list? How did you feel about the values that were added or eliminated? Were there differences of opinion that generated strong feelings in you personally?
3. What values do you hold personally that made this activity easy or difficult?
4. What have you learned?
5. How can you apply information from this experience to your work life?

Debriefing Conclusions

1. While some values may be "normed" as U. S. American, not everyone holds those values, because there are always individual differences within each culture.
2. Cultural values may stem from history, geographical location, economic circumstances, or political dominance.
3. Cultural values that are different from our own are often a source of frustration and misunderstanding.
4. The greater our effort to understand the basis for our cultural differences, the greater the chance for cross-cultural understanding and appreciation.
5. Sometimes the expressed cultural value of a group of people is the same, but the behavior associated with that value within the group is very different. Asking questions can enhance understanding, acceptance, and effectiveness.
6. Finding common ground can assist in developing trust and building understanding.

Adapted from an activity in *The Whole World Guide to Culture Learning* by J. Daniel Hess.

U.S. American Values Handout

Financial security
Freedom of speech
Equality of opportunity
Self-reliance
Patriotism
Tolerance
Freedom of religion
Individual initiative
Private property rights
Government by law
Concern for less fortunate
Fair play
Justice
Social order/stability
Competition
Family

Adapted from an activity in *The Whole World Guide to Culture Learning* by J. Daniel Hess.

25

Performance Evaluations: How Do You Feel? What Do You Think?

Work
L–M
P, O, D, M

Time Required

60 minutes (40 minutes for small-group work; 20 minutes for debriefing)

Objectives

1. To examine different perspectives on the same situation
2. To identify feelings associated with your own perspective
3. To examine the ways your implicit values and/or assumptions influence your perception of the employee performance evaluation process

Materials

- Performance Scenarios Handout for each participant team

Process

1. Place participants in teams of 3–4. Give each participant a copy of the "Performace Scenarios" handout. Assign each team five scenarios.
2. Ask the group to discuss each scenario, using the following questions:
   - How might you feel if you were in this situation as the evaluator? As the employee being evaluated?
   - What assumptions might you make?
   - What expectations would you have?
   - What factors contribute to your feelings, assumptions, and expectations?
   - How might these factors influence your evaluation?
   - How might these factors influence what you communicate—verbally and nonverbally?

Note: These scenarios can be adapted or new ones created to reflect issues pertinent to the organization where the training occurs.

Debriefing Questions

1. Which scenarios were easiest to discuss? Which were the hardest? Why?
2. Were there specific scenarios that generated strong feelings for you? Why?
3. What personal values do you hold that affected your responses to any of the scenarios? To the small-group discussion?
4. What have you learned?
5. How can you apply information from this experience to your work life?

Debriefing Conclusions

1. Dominant cultural values will affect the perceptions, expectations, and anxieties of both the evaluator and the individual being evaluated.
2. It is important for individuals to understand their own values and how those values may influence their assumptions and expectations regarding performance evaluations.
3. Those who are not part of the dominant culture may experience tension and even some resistance to evaluation of their job performance by someone who is part of the dominant culture. Individuals may be apprehensive or nervous, fearing criticism, judgment, or embarrassment.
4. Evaluators may worry about being accurate and fair. They may have concerns about creating conflict or hurting someone's feelings.
5. Considering these differences and their possible impact on the performance review process can help to facilitate a more productive evaluation practice.

Adapted from "Understanding Diversity Blind Spots in the Performance Review" by Anita Rowe.

Performance Scenarios Handout

1. A young male employee is being evaluated by an older female supervisor.

2. An American-born manager is being evaluated by a German-born supervisor.

3. A female engineer with multiple sclerosis is being evaluated by a younger, able-bodied male executive.

4. A male Latino employee, with fifteen years' service, is being evaluated by a female manager who has recently been hired to run the department.

5. A Japanese accountant is being evaluated by a supervisor who was responsible for reassigning another Japanese accountant to a less-respected position.

6. A young female computer programmer is being evaluated by an older male supervisor who has recently been assigned to this department.

7. A Dutch career specialist is being evaluated by the owner of an employment agency that specializes in placement of professional women.

8. A U.S.-born teen, working in a coffee shop, is being evaluated by a Russian-born supervisor.

9. A U.S. manager is evaluating employees in a newly opened retail store in Japan.

10. An older female supervisor is temporarily assigned to the production floor of an aircraft plant. Her assignment is to evaluate the individual contributions of each employee.

11. A female employee, working with a "green card," is being evaluated by an older American-born manager.

12. A middle-aged male engineer is being evaluated by a younger supervisor from the company that has recently merged with his organization.

13. A newly hired personnel manager is evaluating an intact work team in a health-care facility.

14. In a dot-com acquisition, the new department manager is providing yearly performance feedback to program designers.

15. A new supervisor with an MBA from a prestigious university is evaluating a supervisor with fifteen years' experience but no college degree.

Adapted from "Understanding Diversity Blind Spots in the Performance Review" by Anita Rowe.

26

What Is the Message?

Time Required

35 minutes (5 minutes for briefing; 15 minutes for activity; 15 minutes for debriefing)

Objectives

1. To provide experience with different verbal and nonverbal styles of communication
2. To practice describing communication behaviors objectively
3. To discuss subjective responses to a range of communication behaviors that may be different from one's own
4. To begin to identify how communication styles support values

Materials

- 3 x 5 cards with one rule of behavior from the Etiquette Sheet on each card
- A room where participants can move about freely during the activity

Process

1. Using the "Etiquette Sheet" on page 94, type or write each behavior listed on a separate 3 x 5 card. (You may also add etiquette behaviors from your experience or from a specific culture being explored in the workshop.)
2. Supply each participant with one of the 3 x 5 cards. Ask participants *not* to show their cards to each other.
3. Have participants organize themselves into groups of 4–6 and ask them to begin a five-minute conversation on how they hope to use what they will learn today—or any other topic relevant to the session being conducted. Tell the group that each person is to follow the rule from his or her etiquette card.

   Note: Having participants form their own groups allows for discussion about how they made group choices. An optional method, which will take less time, is for you to create the first groups.

4. After five minutes ask people to move to a new group and begin a second conversation (same topic). After another five minutes, ask

people to move to a third group and begin another new conversation (again, same topic). After five minutes stop the conversations and ask participants to return to their seats. Begin the debriefing.

Debriefing Questions

1. What happened during the formation of the original groups? During the first conversation? During the second conversation? During the third conversation? Watch for descriptions of behaviors, not interpretations of those behaviors.

   Note: When interpretations occur, provide an example of a description for that interpretation, then ask participants to limit themselves to descriptions.

2. How did you feel about what you experienced during the group formations? Were you able to identify most of the etiquette rules from members' behavior? How did you feel about any specific etiquette rule you encountered during the conversations? What was the most difficult etiquette rule for you? How did you feel when the activity ended? Why do you think you felt that way?

3. What values might be demonstrated by the different etiquette-related behaviors you exhibited or observed? Which different behaviors may support the same value (e.g., both direct eye contact and avoided eye contact can be intended to demonstrate respect)?

4. What have you learned during this experience?

5. How can you apply information from this experience to your everyday life?

Debriefing Conclusions

1. We usually seek out people with whom we have some history or perceived similarities.

2. It is easier to interpret behavior from our own perspective than to objectively describe it.

3. The same values can be demonstrated with a range of different behaviors.

4. Interpreting others' behaviors from our own perspective may lead to the wrong conclusion.

5. In the workplace, wrong conclusions may lead to misinterpretations, ineffective behaviors, or conflict.

Optional/Additional Debriefing Questions

1. What happened?
   - Were there differences between your conversation in the first group and in the second group? Why do you think those differences occurred?

   Note: Participants may have gravitated to people they were comfortable with during the first group formation and may have had less choice thereafter.

   - Were you tempted to reveal the contents of your etiquette card? Did you want to ask others about the content of theirs?

- Did you mistake someone's behavior as his or her natural behavior when it was actually what he or she had been instructed to do?
2. How did you feel?
   - What made you feel most embarrassed during the conversations? Why?
   - Which behavior did you consider to be the rudest or most offensive? Why?
3. What have you learned?
   - There is more to a conversation than just words and sentences. Do you agree or disagree with this statement? Why?
   - Sometimes you may feel negative about another person without being aware of it. This is probably because you are disturbed by his or her conversational style. Do you agree or disagree with this statement? Why?
   - Other than the content of the conversation, what factors attracted your attention or made it hard for you to pay attention?
4. How does this relate to the real world?
   - What real-world object or processes do the etiquette rules represent?
   - Have you ever met a person whose conversational style distracted you from paying attention to what he or she was saying? What did you do?
   - Can you think of any of your conversational behaviors that your colleagues could find distracting or strange? Can you think of any of your conversational behaviors that people from other countries (or cultures) might find distracting or strange?
5. What if?
   - What would have happened if the conversations had lasted for 45 minutes (instead of 5 minutes)?
   - What would happen if you were asked to conduct a business meeting with other members of the large group?

Adapted from an activity presented by Sivasailam Thiagarajan at The Summer Institute for Intercultural Communication, 2000.

Etiquette Sheet

It is impolite to be blunt and tactless. It is preferable to talk in abstractions and to approach subjects in an indirect fashion.

It is impolite to speak impulsively. Whenever somebody asks you a question, silently count to seven before you give the answer.

It is impolite to be aloof, so stand close to others until you nearly touch them. If someone backs away, keep moving closer.

It is impolite to crowd people, so maintain your distance—allow at least an arm's length between you and the nearest person. If anyone gets too close to you, back away until you have achieved the required distance.

It is impolite to shout, so talk softly, even whisper. Even if people cannot hear you, do not raise your voice.

It is impolite to talk to more than one person at the same time. Always talk to a single individual standing near to you so that you can have a private conversation. Do not address your remarks to the group as a whole.

It is impolite to stare at people, so avoid eye contact. Look at the floor or the speaker's shoes, not at his or her face.

It is important to get people's attention before you speak. Hold your hand above your head and snap your fingers. Do this every time prior to making a statement or asking a question. That is the polite way to get everyone's attention.

Be yourself! Behave as you would normally behave at an informal party.

It is considered friendly to share your thoughts and feelings without any inhibition. Be sure to make several self-disclosing statements, describing your intimate feelings about different subjects. Ask personal questions of other members of the group.

It is polite and reassuring to reach out and touch someone you are having a conversation with. Touch people on the arm or the shoulder when you speak to them.

It is important to show your enthusiasm. Jump in before other speakers have finished their sentences and add your ideas. Remember, it is rude to hold back your thoughts.

Adapted from an activity presented by Sivasailam Thiagarajan at The Summer Institute for Intercultural Communication, 2000.

27

Visible and Invisible Values

Time Required

60 minutes (15 minutes for lecturette; 20 minutes for activity; 25 minutes for debriefing)

Objectives

1. To examine the relationship between values and behaviors
2. To identify how unconscious assumptions regarding behavior can contribute to cross-cultural misunderstanding
3. To discuss how behavior might be misinterpreted in both positive and negative ways
4. To illustrate the importance of suspending interpretation or judgment until the significance of the behavior within the context of a given culture is understood

Materials

- Visible and Invisible Values Worksheet
- Visible and Invisible Values Alternative Interpretation Worksheet
- Flipchart and marking pens

Process

1. Conduct a brief lecturette (15 minutes) or discussion regarding the visible and invisible aspects of culture (see "Culture and Values Narrative," Appendix A, page 231). Focus on values as an invisible aspect of culture that determine how we act. Differentiate between terminal values (the ultimate goal) and instrumental values (the behaviors that help achieve the goal).
2. Provide all participants with a "Visible and Invisible Values" worksheet and give them approximately 5 minutes to complete it.
3. Put participants in pairs or groups of 3 and give them the "Visible and Invisible Values Alternative Interpretation" worksheet. Ask each group to generate alternative explanations for each behavior. Give them approximately 15 minutes for this process.
4. Bring the groups back together and ask for their alternative explanations for several behaviors.
5. List these on a flipchart.

Note: You need not do all of the behaviors; 2–4 of them will be sufficient for the learning intended.

Debriefing Questions

1. What happened? What was easiest to do? What was hardest? Why?
2. How did you feel as you were matching the values and behaviors? As you were thinking of alternative explanations for each behavior?
3. How did your own values affect your ability to come up with alternative explanations?
4. What have you learned?
5. How would you apply this to your everyday life?

Debriefing Conclusions

1. There are multiple interpretations of behavior. Misinterpretation can cause misunderstanding and/or conflict. The more possible explanations you can think of for a behavior, the more likely you are to identify the accurate one.
2. The stronger one's own values on a subject are, the more difficult it may be to see alternatives.
3. To interpret behavior correctly, it is important to suspend judgment until one has more clarity on the significance of the behavior for the other person.
4. Understanding the cultural context of a behavior will contribute to understanding its meaning.

Adapted from an activity in *Figuring Foreigners Out: A Practical Guide* by Craig Storti.

Visible and Invisible Values Worksheet

Understanding the relationship between values and behaviors is the basis for cross-cultural understanding. Below is a list of values or beliefs on the left and behaviors on the right. Match each value or belief with a behavior that someone holding that value is likely to exhibit.

	Values		Behaviors
1.	Being direct	_____	Use of understatement
2.	Centrality of family	_____	Asking people to call you by your first name
3.	Progress and change	_____	Someone stops at your desk and chats with you every morning but not about work
4.	Fatalism	_____	Taking off work to attend the funeral of a cousin
5.	Saving face	_____	Not asking for help from the person next to you on an exam
6.	Respect for age	_____	Disagreeing openly with someone at a meeting
7.	Informality	_____	Not terminating an older worker whose performance is weak
8.	Deference to authority	_____	At a meeting, agreeing with a suggestion you think is wrong
9.	Present time orientation	_____	Insisting on following rules even when they do not make sense in the situation
10.	Being indirect	_____	Inviting the tea boy to eat lunch with you in your office
11.	Relationship oriented	_____	Insisting on trying new ways of doing things even though the old way is working perfectly well
12.	Self-reliance	_____	Asking the boss' opinion on something you are an expert on
13.	Egalitarianism	_____	Accepting, without question, that something cannot be changed
14.	Fixed rules	_____	Consistently being late to meetings because of conversations in the hallway on the way to the meeting

Adapted from an activity in *Figuring Foreigners Out: A Practical Guide* by Craig Storti.

Visible and Invisible Values Alternative Interpretation Worksheet

Any behavior can have multiple explanations—especially when viewed across cultural differences. Below is the list of behaviors you have already examined. On this page you are asked to work with your partner or group to identify at least one explanation for each behavior that is different from the one identified on the Visible and Invisible Values Worksheet.

Behaviors	Possible Alternative Explanations
Use of understatement	_____ _____
Asking people to call you by your first name	_____ _____
Someone stops at your desk and chats with you every morning but not about work	_____ _____
Taking off work to attend the funeral of a cousin	_____ _____
Not asking for help from the person next to you on an exam	_____ _____
Disagreeing openly with someone at a meeting	_____ _____
Not terminating an older worker whose performance is weak	_____ _____

At a meeting, agreeing with a suggestion you think is wrong

_____

_____

Insisting on following rules even when they do not make sense in the situation

_____

_____

Inviting the tea boy to eat lunch with you in your office

_____

_____

Insisting on trying new ways of doing things even though the old way is working perfectly well

_____

_____

Asking the boss' opinion on something you are an expert on

_____

_____

Accepting, without question, that something cannot be changed

_____

_____

Consistently being late to meetings because of conversations in the hallway on the way to the meeting

_____

_____

Adapted from an activity in *Figuring Foreigners Out: A Practical Guide* by Craig Storti.

28

Similarities and Differences

Time Required

35–40 minutes (20 minutes for playing, 15–20 minutes for debriefing)

Objectives

1. To discover similarities and differences between and among people
2. To identify those differences that require little effort to discover and those that require extra effort
3. To identify how assumed similarities or differences can restrict our use of the resources and/or opportunities other people can provide us

Materials

None

Process

1. Ask participants to form groups with others who have some *visible* similarities with themselves. Ask the groups to identify one thing they value about the similarity or similarities around which they have formed. Allow 3 minutes for forming the groups and identifying the trait or attribute they value and why they value that trait; that is, what the similarity represents for them. Ask each group to quickly call out the similarity or similarities around which they have formed and the one thing they value about that similarity (or those similarities).

2. Ask participants to form groups with others who are *visibly* different from them. Ask the groups to identify one thing they value about the difference(s) around which they have formed. Allow 3 minutes for forming the groups and identifying the difference(s) they value. Ask each group to quickly call out the differences around which they have formed and the one thing they value about that difference.

3. Ask participants to form groups with others who are similar to them in some *invisible* way, for example, educational background, religion, or occupation. Ask the groups to identify one thing they value about the similarity or similarities around which they have formed. Allow 5 minutes for forming the group and identifying the

value. Ask each group to quickly call out the similarity or similarities around which they have formed and the one thing they value about that similarity.

4. Ask participants to form groups with others who are different from them in some *invisible* way, for example, educational background, religion, or occupation. Ask the groups to identify one thing they value about the difference(s) around which they have formed. Allow 5 minutes for forming the group and identifying the value. Ask each group to quickly call out the difference(s) around which they have formed and the one thing they value about that difference.

Debriefing Questions

1. What happened? Which groups were easier to form? Why? Which groups were harder to form? Why?
2. How did you feel during this process? Why?
3. What values might have contributed to the groups you formed?
4. What have you learned?
5. How can you apply this information to your everyday life?

Debriefing Conclusions

1. First impressions are often based on visible similarities or differences.
2. Invisible similarities or differences are often more important than those that are visible.
3. We have many similarities with people who look different from us and many differences from people who look similar to us.
4. If we form impressions based only on what is visible, we may miss important skills, characteristics, or perspectives another person could offer us.
5. Those things we feel are important about ourselves—both visible and invisible—are often based on values we hold.

29

If This Is a Value, What Will You See?

Work
M
O, T

Time Required

75 minutes (15 minutes for lecturette; 5 minutes for participants to fill out the worksheet; 15 minutes for group discussion; 10 minutes to prepare newsprint sheets; 30 minutes for debriefing)

Objectives

1. To provide an opportunity to explore organizational values
2. To identify different behaviors that might reflect the same value
3. To facilitate the discussion of values from different perspectives
4. To identify and discuss how value differences can help or hinder effectiveness in a team

Materials

- If This Is a Value, What Will You See? Worksheet for each participant*
- Edward T. Hall transparency and an overhead projector
- A flipchart, pens, and tape for each team

Process

1. Read the Edward T. Hall quote (see transparency master on page 106) and show it as a transparency. Give a lecturette about culture and values (see "Culture and Values Narrative," Appendix A, page 231).
2. Distribute the "If This Is a Value, What Will You See?" worksheet to all of the participants. Ask everyone to read each value statement and to write descriptions of one or two behaviors exemplifying each value that one might observe in an organization that holds this value.
3. Divide the group into teams of 5–7 members. Ask team members to share their behavioral statements. Allow time for a discussion of the similarities and differences in behaviors identified.
4. During group discussion or prior to the workshop, label 8 easel pages, each one with a statement from the worksheet. Divide each page in half with a vertical line. Label one side "Agreed-upon Behaviors" and

---

*   Option: This worksheet can be modified by substituting the organization's stated values.

the other side, "Behaviors Not Agreed to." Tape easel pages around the room. Ask each team to list 1–3 behaviors that the team members agreed upon as reflecting the value from the worksheet and 1–3 behaviors that they did not agree on. Allow time for participants to walk around and read all of the team responses.

Debriefing Questions

1. For which values were behaviors easiest to identify? Why? Which were most difficult? Why?
2. How did this process feel? What is your reaction to the values/behaviors identified as most common/most uncommon in the organization?
3. If one of your behaviors was not commonly agreed upon, what implications might this have for you at work?
4. Which of these values are most easily expressed behaviorally in the workplace? Why?
5. What have you learned?
6. How can you apply what you have learned to your everyday work life?

Debriefing Conclusions

1. Different people might express the same value in a behaviorally different way.
2. If someone expresses a value differently from the "norm" in the organization, they may not be seen as supporting that value.
3. The more an organization's values are defined behaviorally, the more likely everyone is to know what is expected and to agree on the expected behavior.
4. Unless organizational values are expressed in behavioral expectations, individuals can make errors and be seen as acting "inappropriately."
5. The more broadly an organization defines its behavioral expectations, the more people can meet those expectations without giving up who they are as individuals.

If This Is a Value, What Will You See? Worksheet

The following statements reflect certain values or beliefs expressed in some organizations. Please list one or two behaviors that you might observe in an organization that holds this value.

1. Customer satisfaction is a top priority.

   _____

   _____

2. Open communication and collaboration are very important.

   _____

   _____

3. Innovation and creativity are the keys to success.

   _____

   _____

4. Diversity contributes to a competitive advantage.

   _____

   _____

5. Feedback is an important factor in facilitating improvement.

   _____

   _____

6. It is important to celebrate success.

   _____

   _____

7. Strong leadership is an important component of motivation.

   _____

   _____

8. This is a learning organization.

   _____

   _____

"Culture hides much more than it reveals, and strangely enough what it hides, it hides most effectively from its own participants. Years of study have convinced me that the real job is not to understand foreign culture but to understand our own."

—Edward T. Hall (1959), 15

30

Values in Action

Work

M

T, O, D

Time Required

90 minutes (15 minutes for participants to individually identify values; 30 minutes for small-group work; 15 minutes for individual identification of behaviors; 30 minutes for debriefing)

Objectives

1. To identify the explicit and implicit values of the organization
2. To identify behaviors that could support the organizational values
3. To identify behaviors that might not support the organizational values
4. To discuss the possibilities of misinterpretation of the intent of behavior
5. To discuss the impact of behavior that appears incongruent with organizational values

Materials

- Sets of organizational material for review, one for each participant
- Organizational Values Handout for each participant
- Flipchart
- Tape
- Sticky notes
- Medium-sized sticky dots
- Marking pens, pens, pencils

Process

1. Give each participant a copy of the organization's vision and mission statement and the "Organizational Values" handout.
2. Ask participants to read over the company-generated material (other organizational material may be included, e.g., marketing tools, customer service protocols) in an effort to identify the implicit as well as explicit values of the organization. Ask participants to circle any value on the "Organizational Values" that they see reflected in the organization's written materials.
3. The facilitator will have an easel chart or overhead transparency showing the same values as those on the "Organizational Values"

handout. This easel should be in front of the room where everyone can see it.

4. Place participants into groups of 4–6. Ask the groups to discuss their individual choices and come to a consensus on a "top ten" list: those values they all agree are most important as reflected in the written materials. Give each group ten dots for one representative to place next to their ten choices on your values chart (or, if you use an overhead transparency, ask the group representatives to mark their choices with hash marks on the transparency). After each group has indicated their choices, the highest-priority values for the organization should be evident.

Note: If there is no consensus, this will provide an opportunity to direct the training toward the importance of values clarity and how lack of values clarity affects performance and job satisfaction. The participants should then be directed to identify ways to achieve greater clarity in organizational values.

5. Now give each participant 20 sticky notes. Ask everyone to identify, individually, one behavior that he or she thinks would support each of the top ten values and one behavior that would not and to write these behaviors on their sticky notes—one behavior per note.

6. While the participants are writing behaviors, tape up ten sheets of easel paper. Write one of the top ten values at the top of each page, then below the value write "Supportive Behaviors" on one side of the page and "Nonsupportive Behaviors" on the other side of the page.

7. Ask participants to place their sticky notes on the value sheets around the room. Give them time to wander around the room and read the behaviors that others have identified. Tell them to specifically look for any behaviors that might appear to be in conflict. For example, "quick, efficient checkout" might be seen as a behavior that supports good customer service while someone else might see this same behavior as nonsupportive because it may be perceived as unfriendly. What is viewed as fast and efficient service in a U.S. restaurant might be interpreted by some Europeans as an attempt to rush the meal and get on to the next customer.

Debriefing Questions

1. Answer the following:
   - Are the values of the organization clear from the written materials?
   - Are the behaviors of people within the organization supportive of the values in the written materials? If not, how might this affect managers, employees, or customers?
   - Where was it easiest or hardest for the small groups and large group to come to agreement on the top ten values? Why?
   - Was it easy or difficult for the group to agree on behaviors that support a value? Why?
2. How did you feel during this process? Why?

3. Which actions or behaviors among your group members were helpful to you as you worked together? What values were demonstrated in the way you held your discussion? Were there behaviors that helped or hindered your group participation? What values do you hold that made those behaviors helpful or hindering?
4. What have you learned?
   • What happens if we both have the same value but behave in different ways to demonstrate that value?
   • What strategies might we use to resolve those differences?
   • What happens if your personal values are inconsistent with those of the organization?
   • What strategies might you use to manage those differences?
5. How could you apply information from this activity to your work life?

Debriefing Conclusions

1. Individual actions are not always in alignment with organizational values.
2. Actions can speak louder than words.
3. A wide range of actions may demonstrate the same organizational value.
4. The intent behind someone's behavior may not match the interpretation of that behavior by the receiver. It is important to ask questions that will clarify intent.
5. Actions that are seen and understood as congruent with organizational values foster trust and promote authenticity.

Adapted from an activity in *Personal Workbook: Understanding and Working with Values* by Brian P. Hall.

Organizational Values Handout

1. **Accountability/Ethics**: Recognizing managers and employees for behaviors that support the written values. This might be through bonus or performance review systems, through recognition ceremonies, or in other ways that acknowledge those who behave consistently with the organization's stated values or ethics.

2. **Achievement/Success**: Acknowledging and rewarding those who meet individual and/or team targets.

3. **Adaptability/Flexibility**: Adjusting readily to changing business conditions and challenges; remaining flexible even under stressful circumstances.

4. **Administration/Control**: Managing systems and processes of the organization's activities.

5. **Belief/Philosophy**: Supporting the beliefs that are essential to the success of the organization.

6. **Change**: Supporting ongoing transformation of the organization in order to prosper in the world of business, enhance the quality of life, create meaningful work for all employees, and develop an institution that benefits society.

7. **Collaboration**: Cooperating with all levels of the organization to achieve success and serve customers.

8. **Communication/Information**: Transmitting ideas and information among persons, departments, and divisions of the organization effectively and efficiently. This includes efficient use of meetings, e-mail, phones, facsimile, and memoranda.

9. **Commitment/Cooperation**: Attaining sufficient commitment to the organization and its members so that interdependent cooperation is achieved.

10. **Competition**: Possessing a positive sense of challenge to be first and most respected in a given arena. Emphasis is on being competitive with oneself—to be the best one can.

11. **Control/Order/Discipline**: Providing restraint, direction, and professional discipline to achieve success according to prescribed rules.

12. **Creativity/Innovation**: Introducing creative ideas for positive change in business and social organizations and systems. This includes developing new products and services that are responsive to client and customer needs and providing a framework for actualizing them.

13. **Discernment**: Enabling a group or organization to achieve consensus in long-term planning decisions through openness, reflection, and honest interaction.

14. **Education**: Encouraging and providing support for employees to complete the education and training they need to continually improve their capabilities.

15. **Hierarchy/Order**: Recognizing the essential and positive nature of layered management that conforms to established standards of what is proper within an organization.

16. **Human Dignity**: Encouraging systems and practices that actively support consciousness of the basic right of every person to have respect and to have basic needs met. Beyond this, there is a need for management structures and practices that empower employees, customers, and stakeholders with the opportunity to develop their potential through mutual accountability, collaboration, and personal/professional development.

17. **Inclusiveness**: To be open to—and value—different points of view regardless of gender, cultural origin, or perspective.

18. **Independence**: Encouraging individuals to think and act for themselves without always being subject to external constraints or authority.

19. **Mutual Accountability**: Maintaining a reciprocal balance of tasks and assignments so that everyone is answerable for his or her own area of responsibility. This requires the ability to manage conflict and deal with differences in creative and supportive ways that move relationships to increasing levels of cooperation.

20. **Prestige/Image:** Promoting an organizational style and appearance that reflects success and achievement, gains the esteem of others, and promotes success.

21. **Productivity:** Feeling energized by generating and completing tasks and by achieving established goals and expectations.

22. **Reason:** Facilitating a team, group, or individuals to think logically and reasonably, even under stress, in a way that is based on a formal body of information. This is the capacity to exercise reason before emotions, while still taking emotions seriously.

23. **Research:** Systematically collecting and analyzing data for the purpose of creating new insights, products, and service.

24. **Safety/Survival:** Guarding the safety of all personnel against personal injury and danger or loss by doing what is necessary to set up systems and procedures to support this end.

25. **Technology:** Prioritizing resources and technology as a significant part of business.

26. **Tradition:** Ritualizing history and traditions as an important link from the past to the future. Recognizing corporate history as a way of enriching the meaning of what the organization stands for.

27. **Unity/Diversity:** Recognizing that an organization is creatively enhanced by giving equal opportunity to persons from a variety of cultures, ethnic backgrounds, and education. The concept is that differences are an advantage in a collaborative learning environment.

28. **Workmanship/Art/Craft:** Encouraging capabilities requiring manual dexterity to produce artifacts and/or technology that enhance the quality of life for ourselves and our customers.

Adapted from an activity in *Personal Workbook: Understanding and Working with Values* by Brian P. Hall.

31

Sorting Values

Adaptable

M

P, T, O, D, M

Time Required

60 minutes (10 minutes for small groups; 10 minutes to record results; 40 minutes for debriefing)

Objectives

1. To identify values that are shared by group members
2. To identify values that are not commonly held by all group members
3. To explore ways that difference may foster misunderstanding
4. To examine how values contribute to or interfere with effective organizational behavior
5. To identify how the organization or team can maximize the benefits of values that are shared and the benefits of those that are not

Materials

- A watch with a second hand or a stopwatch for each group
- A Values Questions Worksheet for each small group
- Flipchart

Process

1. Ask participants to form groups of 4 and to choose one member to serve as the questioner/recorder. Give these questioners/recorders a copy of the "Values Questions" worksheet and a watch with a second hand or a stopwatch. Ask these individuals to read each question to their group and to record how many seconds it takes for the other 3 members to agree on a yes or no answer.

   Note: There is no place to record participant answers because they aren't important. The key is how long it took the group to come to agreement.

   Note: Participants may ask whether they are to answer these questions as if they were at work or at home. Point out that our values don't change just because we change location, although our behaviors—the way we exhibit our values—can change when we go into different settings. Therefore, encourage people to think broadly about how they would respond to these questions. If you experience resistance, encourage them to think about themselves at work, since this is the context in which they are exploring the issues. You may also want to return to this question during debriefing by asking participants how they would have answered things differently for "not at work." Use this as an opportunity to examine aspects of the work environment that discourage the acknowledgment of one's personal values in that environment.

Note also that the values questions can be modified or questions can be deleted or added based on what is happening in the work environment where you are conducting this activity.

2. While the groups are at work, make up a newsprint chart (or you could prepare handouts ahead of time) for recording group results. The first column will list the questions by number with the primary value on the "Values Questions" worksheet. The second column will list the small groups by number. The third column will be for the recording of small-group agreement times.

Question #	Small Group #	Seconds to agreement
1 (Persistence)	1	2.2
	2	2.3
	3	2.1
	4	2.2
	5	2.7
2 (Courtesy)	1	2.7
	2	5.1
	3	7.2
	4	3.9
	5	8.3

3. After the small groups have answered all of the questions, the questioners/recorders will record on the newsprint chart the time it took to reach agreement on each question.

4. Using two criteria, the length of time it took the groups to come to agreement and the number of groups that agreed, examine the values that are shared by participants. As you can see from the sample above, there is pretty strong agreement about persistence, while courtesy was a much more difficult question on which to come to agreement.

Debriefing Questions

1. What values were easy to agree on? Which ones were difficult? Why?

2. How did you feel about your group's interactions? Decisions? How did you feel when a consensus could not be reached, or when reaching it took longer than you felt it should?

3. Which of your values were most challenged during this process? Why? How did you respond when this happened?

4. What have you learned from your experience today? Which values were most consistent across the small groups? Which ones were most inconsistent? How might these consistencies or inconsistencies affect

workplace relationships? Productivity? Communication? Conflict?

5. How could you apply information from this activity to your work life? How can you use the consistencies or inconsistencies to strengthen the organization or team?

Debriefing Conclusions

1. Not all people share the same values—or place the same importance on values they might actually have in common.
2. Individuals bring their values to work with them and act on them on a daily basis—although not always consciously.
3. Values differences can affect individual and organizational effectiveness.
4. Examining values can foster clarity about differences.
5. Understanding different points of view may be grounds for future cooperation and collaboration.

Alternate Process

By creating small groups that are segregated by gender, race/ethnicity, job title, age, or other demographic groupings important in the organization or team being trained, you could talk about why these values differences might exist and how the organization or team can develop operational norms that will reduce potential conflicts and maximize the resource of values differences among the groups.

Adapted from research described by Harry C. Triandis for *Culture and Social Behavior*, published in 1994 by McGraw-Hill.

Values Questions Worksheet

Question	Time to Agree
1. Is it important to persist until you have completed a job?	
2. Is it important to practice common courtesies with others?	
3. Is it important to be cautious when making decisions?	
4. Is it important to be adaptable, to change when things aren't working?	
5. Is it important to be patient with others?	
6. Is it important to be in close harmony with the environment and other people?	
7. Is it important to take advantage of opportunities?	
8. Is it important to be compassionate and to forgive others?	
9. Is it important to balance action, reflection, feelings, and thoughts?	
10. Is it important to be thrifty?	
11. Is it important to tolerate others' differences?	
12. Is it important to be self-reliant and independent?	
13. Is it important to value the past through traditions or rituals?	
14. Is it important to be respectful and obedient to parents?	
15. Is it important to acknowledge other people's status?	
16. Is it important to meet your commitments, to be reliable?	
17. Is it important to have a sense of righteousness?	
18. Is it important to be happy?	
19. Is it important to be close to others, to have a sense of intimacy?	
20. Is it important to have a close family?	
21. Is it important to be patriotic?	
22. Is it important to be loyal?	
23. Is it important to be moderate in your behaviors?	
24. Is it important to have a high income so you can do what you want?	
25. Is it important to use your skills to achieve success?	

Adapted from research described by Harry C. Triandis for *Culture and Social Behavior,* published in 1994 by McGraw-Hill.

32

Leading Values

Time Required

90–120 minutes (30 minutes for individual work; 30 minutes for small-group discussion; 30–60 minutes for debriefing and development of organizational action plans)

Objectives

1. To recognize values as our personal motivators, giving meaning and purpose to our actions
2. To explore behaviors of leaders that inspire others to strive for excellence
3. To see how an organization can focus on shared values as a path to identifying leadership skills that will be most effective within the organization

Materials

- A copy of the Leading Values List for each participant
- A flipchart and marking pen
- A copy of the Leadership Styles Handout for each participant
- 5 index cards for each participant
- Pens or pencils for participants
- Tape

Process

1. In preparation for this activity, make a newsprint sheet for each of the leadership styles listed in the "Leadership Styles" handout. Write the style at the top of the page and post all four pages on the walls around the room. Provide each participant with a copy of the "Leading Values" list and five blank index cards.
2. Ask participants to carefully review the "Leading Values" list and to identify the five most important values for them at work—those values that motivate them to quality performance.
3. Instruct participants to write one of their five selected values on each index card. On the back of the card, ask them to also list three behaviors or actions that they assume a leader who held this same value would exhibit.

4. Distribute the "Leadership Styles" handout, which also lists each style's accompanying behaviors. Give participants time to study these lists to determine which of their cards should go with which leadership style.

5. Tell participants that when they are ready, they are to tape each of their five values cards on the newsprint page of the leadership style that they believe would be most likely to exhibit the behaviors they have listed as demonstrating that value.

   Note: Many values will "fit" under several of the leadership styles. The distinguishing factors are most likely to be the associated behaviors. For example, respect can be shown by a transactional leader taking care of your basic needs or by a situational leader including you in decision making. Vision can be shared through the chain of command by a transactional leader or collaboratively developed by a transformational leader. The facilitator will need to help participants make these types of distinctions as they decide where to place their values cards.

6. Ask participants to form four groups, with each group responsible for discussing one of the leadership styles. Each group will take the newsprint page associated with their assigned style along with the 3 x 5 values cards taped to it and discuss the behaviors and their underlying values as under their assigned style, using these questions as guides:
   • What themes emerge in either common values or common behaviors expected from leaders using this style?
   • Are there any inconsistencies in either the values or behaviors expected of this leadership style?
   • What type of employee (that is, what values or behavior expectations) might this leadership style have difficulty in motivating?

7. Instruct the small groups to return to the larger group and ask each small group to report the results of their discussion.

Debriefing Questions

1. What was the easiest part of this exercise for you to do? Hardest? Where was the consistency or inconsistency in expectations of each leadership style? What common themes did you hear either within or across leadership styles?

2. What feelings emerged for you as you participated in this activity? In the small-group discussions?

3. What values does this organization hold that would support or fail to support each of these leadership styles? If the organization is to achieve success, given its values and industry context, which leadership style(s) might best motivate employees to sustain its efforts? Why?

4. What have you learned?

5. How could you apply information from this experience to your work life?

Debriefing Conclusions

1. Individuals are motivated by different values in the workplace.
2. The same value can be demonstrated by similar or different behaviors.
3. Leadership behaviors are interpreted as supportive or not supportive primarily based on values held by employees.
4. When leadership behaviors are interpreted as supporting employees' values, employees are most likely to be motivated to achieve quality performance.
5. When leadership behaviors support the organization's values, organizational goals are most likely to be met and sustained.

Optional Debriefing Questions

This activity will be most effective if used with leaders from the same organization. The following additional debriefing questions become a plan of action for the organization.

1. What leadership behaviors will most support the stated values of this organization? Why?
2. What skill sets will leaders need to translate these values into related behaviors?
3. How might we assess the skill level of each leader in the organization in each value area?
4. What support, coaching, and training can we provide each leader for those areas needing improvement?
5. How will we communicate these changes to employees so they know what the organization's leaders are doing to develop the necessary skills to support employees and the organization's values?

Adapted from an activity in *Building Cultures of Excellence: Getting Started with Values* by Brian P. Hall and Martin L. W. Hall.

Leading Values List

Accountability

Achievement/Success

Change

Compassion

Competition

Control

Cooperation

Courtesy

Creativity/Innovation

Discipline/Order

Duty/Obligation

Education

Equality

Financial Security

Flexibility

Friendship

Generosity

Global Justice

Group Unity

Harmony

Hierarchy/Order

Higher Order/Spiritual Connection

Honesty

Honor

Independence

Laws/Rules

Learning/Personal Growth

Loyalty

Mentorship/Nurturance

Obedience/Duty

Patience

Prestige/Image

Productivity

Quality Work

Recreation/Pleasure

Respect

Responsibility

Security

Solitude

Tradition

Vision

Adapted from an activity in *Building Cultures of Excellence: Getting Started with Values* by Brian P. Hall and Martin L. W. Hall.

Leadership Styles Handout

Transactional Leader

- Works within the status quo of the organization
- Works with her or his constituents in the way they most prefer
- Bargains and exchanges one thing for another
- Establishes clear goals and expectations
- Monitors deviance from standards
- Takes action only when necessary

Transformational Leader

- Works to change the organization
- Is a reformer
- Seeks to satisfy a higher need or purpose
- Helps others understand the big picture
- Motivates employees to do more than is expected and to desire success
- Involves employees in decision making
- Models, coaches, mentors, and creates learning opportunities
- Thinks "outside the box" and encourages subordinates to do the same

Transforming Leader

- Helps subordinates take leadership roles
- Stimulates subordinates to develop professionally
- Helps subordinates learn new skills
- Helps subordinates become leaders

Situational Leader

- Changes behaviors based on the situation
- Includes subordinates in decisions
- Helps subordinates develop new skills by coaching them
- Delegates both tasks and responsibilities

Adapted from an activity in *Building Cultures of Excellence: Getting Started with Values* by Brian P. Hall and Martin L. W. Hall.

33

Customer Values

The most successful companies are those that understand what their customers value. Customers are the only ones who can say what will satisfy their wants; it is therefore extremely important for the organization to understand the customer's opinion of what is needed or what is of value. The customer is more likely to spend money with an organization that behaviorally demonstrates a value that is similar to his or her own.

The following activity assumes that the organization *wants to maintain its current customer base* and that the session is being conducted with a group of participants who will ultimately be held responsible for improving service to current customers. If the organization is interested in expanding customer niches, the questions can be modified with the process remaining the same.

Time Required
185 minutes (60 minutes for individual work [Steps 1–5]; 20 minutes for small-group work [Step 6]; 75 minutes for large-group work and discussion [Steps 7–8]; 30 minutes for debriefing)

Objectives
1. To identify who the customer is
2. To identify what the customer values
3. To generate suggestions for more effectively meeting customer needs

Materials
- Flipchart
- Pens, marking pens
- 3 x 5 sticky notepads in three different colors
- Colored sticky dots
- A room with at least three large wall spaces available

Process
1. Explain to the group that your goal is to generate ideas for more effectively meeting customer needs. You will begin by asking them to identify their customers and their customers' values.

2. Provide each participant with three 3 x 5 sticky notepads, each a different color.
3. Ask each participant to identify 2–5 key *characteristics of current customers* and to write these on one color of sticky notes, one statement per note. The statements should be large enough to be seen from several feet away. Ask participants to place those sticky notes on one wall in the room, then *without talking*, to sort the sticky notes into 5–7 related groupings (e.g., physical characteristics, psychological characteristics, demand behavior, etc.). Next, instruct them to place the sticky notes on newsprint sheets with major headings based on the groupings identified. Post those pages with their notes on a wall where they are visible to everyone.
4. Now instruct participants to identify *what they believe to be their customers' values*—keeping the customer identification they have just completed in mind. Again, ask each individual to identify 2–5 key values, then write them separately on sticky notes of a different color, large enough to be seen from several feet away. Ask them to repeat the process of sticking the notes on the wall, sorting the statements into groups (e.g., quality, personal service/relationship, creativity, etc.), and placing the notes on newsprint with major headings based on the groupings identified. Post those pages on a wall that is visible to everyone.
5. Now follow the same procedure with the third color of sticky notes, this time identifying the 2–5 *major areas/issues that they believe the organization could help improve its customer service by addressing*—again keeping in mind the already-identified customer characteristics and values.
6. Assign participants to teams of 3–4, with each team being assigned *one* of the major areas identified for improvement (from the third set of sticky notes). Ask each team to brainstorm a minimum of 10–20 ideas for improvement in their assigned area, then to write their ideas on a flipchart sheet.
7. Call the larger group together and ask each team to present its ideas for improvement. All individuals are provided with three sticky dots for each of the issue areas being explored (e.g., five areas=15 dots per person). After the presentation by each small group, request individuals to place their three dots for that issue on the three ideas they believe would make the greatest and quickest difference in customer service.
8. Once the three top ideas for improvement in each area are identified, ask the large group to decide who will be responsible for implementing the idea and to agree to a follow-up time line for assessing the effectiveness of the strategy.

   Note: This last step is very broadly defined. Because this activity is designed as an actual action activity, the individuals involved in this session will make determinations about implementing strategies, responsibilities, and timelines.

Debriefing Questions

1. Which of these areas (characteristics, values, improvements) were easiest and which were most difficult to identify? Why?
2. How do you feel about your understanding of the customers' values, characteristics, and needs? How do you feel about the processes used to identify customer service weaknesses and the chances for these processes to succeed in improving customer service?
3. What personal values do you hold that will make it either easier or more difficult for you to pursue implementation of the customer service priorities generated?
4. What have you learned?
5. How will you apply information from this experience to your work life? How will you support those responsible for implementation?

Debriefing Conclusions

1. Successful organizations are those that come closest to correctly identifying their customers' needs and wants and then striving to satisfy those needs. This is a challenge for any organization and may be even greater when customers come from a range of cultural groups (ethnic, national, gender, age, etc.)
2. Customers act on their own needs and desires. They will gravitate to whatever organization can meet their needs in a way that supports their values. Beginning with an identification and understanding of customer characteristics and values will usually result in more effective customer service.
3. Strength in performance comes from an alignment of customer, employee, and organizational values and needs.

Optional Process

If the participants do not have responsibility for implementing customer service improvements but can suggest changes to someone else in the organization, the last step in the process would be to "think three": summarize the 3 most important characteristics and the 3 most critical values of their customers, then choose 3 areas of customer service that need to be improved and finally 3 ideas for improvement in each of these areas. This information could then be passed on to the individual or group responsible for implementation.

34

Customer Service Values Survey

Work
M
P, T

Time Required

75 minutes (20 minutes for individual work; 20 minutes for small-group discussion; 35 minutes for debriefing)

Objectives

1. To discern personal values in areas affecting customer service
2. To identify specific customer behaviors (based on values) that will be most challenging
3. To devise strategies for improving customer service in areas that challenge one's personal values

Materials

- A copy of Customer Service Self-Assessment for each participant
- A copy of the Customer Service Self-Assessment Scoring Sheet for each participant
- A copy of the Interpretation of Responses to Customer Service Self-Assessment Handout for each participant

Process

1. Ask each participant to complete the "Customer Service Self-Assessment," then to transfer her or his score for each item to the "Customer Service Self-Assessment Scoring Sheet," and then to tally a total score for each subscale.
2. Provide each participant with an "Interpretation of Responses to Customer Service Self-Assessment" handout and give him or her a few minutes to read the interpretation for each subscale that corresponds to his or her score on that subscale.
3. Instruct participants to form groups of 5–7 or assign them yourself. Ask them to discuss
   - anything they learned or had reinforced about themselves,
   - similarities or differences (in the subscales) from others in the group, and
   - possible ways they might modify their behavior with customers to increase effectiveness.
4. Invite participants to return to the larger group for debriefing.

Debriefing Questions

1. Did you have any new insights? Any areas where your self-perceptions were reinforced?
2. How did you feel about values and behaviors you identified?
3. What values do you hold that might make your current job challenging?
4. What have you learned?
5. How can you apply this information to your workplace? Are there modifications in the job arrangements that could be helpful to your ability to work within your own value system? For example, can you take all or most of the customers who want personal attention while a co-worker manages most of the "back office research"?

Debriefing Conclusions

1. Our values affect the way we prefer to offer customer service and what types of customers we might feel most comfortable with.
2. If there is an inconsistency between our values and our job requirements, it can create personal stress and reduce job effectiveness.
3. Teams can often rearrange work processes to help each individual work in ways that best correspond to his or her values.
4. Teams can provide support for each other in those areas where work requirements and personal preferences might be incongruent.

Optional Process

If the group is an intact work team, consider a discussion about ways in which the team might (a) reorganize their processes to allow each individual greater comfort in serving customers based on the individual's identified values and/or (b) provide each other greater support in those areas where their values might make customer service difficult.

Customer Service Self-Assessment

Our personal values and work preferences can affect our responses to customers. This assessment is an opportunity for you to identify where some of those challenges might occur for you. Please circle your answer to the following questions based on your *most frequent* feelings or behaviors. Please note that *N* is neutral, not "don't know." Each item requires a thoughtful response for effective interpretation. Try to respond regarding your feelings generally as well as how you act in the workplace. Please think about people you serve both outside (external customers) and inside (colleagues, supervisors) your organization.

> *Note: This survey is for general self-assessment only. It has not been statistically validated. Do not use it for personnel decisions.*

For each statement please circle one of the following: SA = strongly agree; A = agree; N = neutral; D = disagree; SD = strongly disagree.

	SA	A	N	D	SD
1. I enjoy serving people who want me to do everything for them.	SA 1	A 2	N 3	D 4	SD 5
2. I prefer customers who are polite, quiet, wait their turn, and thank me.	SA 1	A 2	N 3	D 4	SD 5
3. I show my feelings easily and like working with others who do too.	SA 1	A 2	N 3	D 4	SD 5
4. I don't like working alone and avoid it as much as possible.	SA 5	A 4	N 3	D 2	SD 1
5. I am interested in the ideas of people who don't think like I do.	SA 5	A 4	N 3	D 2	SD 1
6. I consciously try to control my assumptions about people.	SA 5	A 4	N 3	D 2	SD 1
7. I particularly enjoy working with and talking to customers, even when I have other work to do.	SA 1	A 2	N 3	D 4	SD 5
8. I recognize that my way of doing things is not the only way.	SA 5	A 4	N 3	D 2	SD 1
9. I prefer customers who are informal and address me by my first name.	SA 1	A 2	N 3	D 4	SD 5
10. I get annoyed when children behave inappropriately in public places.	SA 1	A 2	N 3	D 4	SD 5
11. Receiving approval or praise is an important factor in my job satisfaction.	SA 5	A 4	N 3	D 2	SD 1
12. I appreciate rules that are flexible and allow me to make decisions based on the situation.	SA 5	A 4	N 3	D 2	SD 1
13. I regularly try to improve my customer service skills.	SA 5	A 4	N 3	D 2	SD 1

14. I dislike conflict, so when I disagree with someone, I usually keep it to myself.	SA 1	A 2	N 3	D 4	SD 5
15. I work best when I can complete a task before being asked to do something else.	SA 1	A 2	N 3	D 4	SD 5
16. If I don't want to do something, I will procrastinate instead of denying the request.	SA 1	A 2	N 3	D 4	SD 5
17. I feel energized when I am busy and I am involved in multiple tasks much of the day.	SA 5	A 4	N 3	D 2	SD 1
18. How others assess my performance is more important to me than how I feel I have done.	SA 5	A 4	N 3	D 2	SD 1
19. I enjoy working with customers who are unclear about what they need and want me to help them clarify their needs.	SA 1	A 2	N 3	D 4	SD 5
20. I get very uncomfortable when I cannot understand someone's speech.	SA 1	A 2	N 3	D 4	SD 5
21. I don't mind listening to and helping a customer who is frustrated or angry, because I don't take it personally.	SA 5	A 4	N 3	D 2	SD 1
22. I prefer working alone.	SA 1	A 2	N 3	D 4	SD 5
23. I prefer to be more formal with customers by addressing them with their title (e.g., Mr. Smith, Dr. Ramos, Ms. Li).	SA 5	A 4	N 3	D 2	SD 1
24. If I don't want to do something, I say no and try to persuade the other person I'm right, if necessary.	SA 5	A 4	N 3	D 2	SD 1
25. I prefer a work environment that is predictable.	SA 1	A 2	N 3	D 4	SD 5
26. I have high, sometimes unreasonable, expectations of others.	SA 1	A 2	N 3	D 4	SD 5
27. I worry that others might take advantage of me unless I am careful.	SA 1	A 2	N 3	D 4	SD 5
28. I am most comfortable when the rules are clear so that I don't have to interpret them but can simply apply them.	SA 1	A 2	N 3	D 4	SD 5
29. It's not easy for me to put myself in someone else's shoes.	SA 1	A 2	N 3	D 4	SD 5
30. I am comfortable using policies to deny a customer request, regardless of their response.	SA 5	A 4	N 3	D 2	SD 1
31. I am most comfortable when my working environment is quiet and orderly.	SA 5	A 4	N 3	D 2	SD 1
32. The customer who demands help without acknowledging me or thanking me bothers me. It feels as if I am being treated like a servant, as inferior.	SA 1	A 2	N 3	D 4	SD 5

33. I prefer working with customers who know exactly what they want and simply need me to direct them to it.	SA 5	A 4	N 3	D 2	SD 1
34. I enjoy working with people who are culturally different from me.	SA 5	A 4	N 3	D 2	SD 1
35. Customers who talk a lot interfere with my getting my work done.	SA 5	A 4	N 3	D 2	SD 1
36. I don't mind working with customers who are demanding.	SA 5	A 4	N 3	D 2	SD 1
37. I feel uncomfortable telling a customer we cannot meet her/his need.	SA 1	A 2	N 3	D 4	SD 5
38. I am a fairly private person and generally keep things to myself.	SA 1	A 2	N 3	D 4	SD 5
39. I appreciate receiving feedback, even if it is negative.	SA 5	A 4	N 3	D 2	SD 1
40. I prefer customers who politely ask for help and thank me for my services. Even if it is my job to serve them, this makes me feel appreciated.	SA 1	A 2	N 3	D 4	SD 5
41. My own assessment of my performance is more important to me than what others think about me.	SA 1	A 2	N 3	D 4	SD 5
42. I am comfortable with frequent changes in my work environment.	SA 5	A 4	N 3	D 2	SD 1
43. I am comfortable with changing technology.	SA 5	A 4	N 3	D 2	SD 1
44. I thrive in an environment where there is a lot of activity, noise, and visual stimuli.	SA 5	A 4	N 3	D 2	SD 1

Customer Service Self-Assessment Scoring Sheet

Subscale	Items in this Subscale	Your Score on Each Item	Total Score for Subscale
1. Preference for working with others	4 22		
2. Preference for an active, stimulating work environment	31 44		
3. Preference for doing things for others	1 19 33		
4. Preference for doing multiple tasks simultaneously	15 17		
5. Preference for flexible rules	12 28		
6. Preference for working with people who are different from yourself	3 5 20 34		
7. Preference for completing tasks	7 35		
8. Comfort level with conflict	2 14 16 21 24 30 36 37		
9. Self-awareness and tolerance	6 8 10 13 26 27 29 38		

Subscale	Items in this Subscale	Your Score on Each Item	Total Score for Subscale
10. Comfort level with ambiguity and/or change	25 42 43		
11. Preference for feedback	11 18 39 41		
12. Preference for status and formality	9 23 32 40		

Interpretation of Responses to Customer Service Self-Assessment Handout

1. *Preference for working with others.* Customer service is often provided by teams, or it may involve working with others to identify solutions to customers' challenges. Customer service can also be provided in a solitary way between the customer and you. This subscale measures the degree to which you prefer either of these situations.

   - 2–4 points. You indicate a preference for working alone. You may be most satisfied with work that allows you to meet the customer's needs without consulting others. Referring customers to others or working in a team to meet customers' needs may be less comfortable or even something you avoid. If you are required to work in a team, it could be helpful to identify solitary tasks and volunteer to do those so that you get an occasional "break" from teamwork.
   - 5–7 points. You indicate no preference for working alone or with others. You can likely adjust to a situation that allows you to make autonomous decisions or one that requires you to work with a team of people to serve customer needs.
   - 8–10 points. You indicate a preference for working with others or being around others. Customer service provided in a team environment will be most enjoyable for you. You may be less satisfied with a customer service job that requires you to serve customers in a solitary fashion, such as work in telephone service centers. If you are in this type of assignment, you may want to identify a team, task force, or other group activity required by your organization and volunteer for those opportunities that might give you the group contact that will feel more satisfying.

2. *Preference for an active, stimulating work environment.* Many customer service situations involve a very public work space that is surrounded by customers and considerable activity and noise. Other customer service situations allow you more control over your personal work space, where things are a bit quieter and more orderly. This subscale identifies which of these situations will be most satisfying for you.

   - 2–4 points. You indicate a preference for a quiet, orderly work environment. Customer service situations that are noisy and have constant interruptions and a lot of stimulation may challenge you or make you nervous. For example, the presence of a lot of noisy children, loud music, or constantly ringing telephones may interfere with your assisting customers comfortably. You may also have conflicts over how to handle situations where you are required to serve both in-person customers and telephone customers, sometimes simultaneously. You could find it helpful to identify how you might reduce the stress of this work environment. For example, can you trade some tasks during the day that will allow you a break from the public customer service work? Is it possible to introduce music that is more soothing? At a minimum, identify quiet places to spend breaks and lunches so you can regenerate your energy.
   - 5–7 points. You indicate no preference for either type of work environment and can likely work in either an active and stimulating environment or one that is more quiet and orderly.
   - 8–10 points. You indicate a preference for a working environment that is active and stimulating. You will do quite well in an open environment where many things are happening simultaneously. You are likely to be most challenged by settings that are quiet and orderly, with very little customer contact or stimulation. If you are working in a quieter setting, consider identifying ways to increase your time in a more public customer service setting.

3. *Preference for doing things for others.* Some customers are indecisive or lack confidence and want you to help them make decisions or take care of their needs without a lot of involvement on their part. Other customers are fairly independent and decisive—they simply want you to help them take care of what they already know they need. Or they may want you to teach them how to use a "system," for instance, library searches or Internet orders, so they can take care of themselves in the future. The items in this subscale identify the degree to which you prefer to work with one of these types of customers.

- 3–6 points. You indicate a preference for doing things for people. You are likely to be most comfortable with customers who want you to help them identify what they need. You may enjoy helping customers make decisions. On the other hand, you will often be challenged by the customer who wants very little help from you. You may also be uncomfortable with customers who want you to explain how to do something. You would rather serve people and play a significant role in helping them than teach them how to serve themselves. You might remind yourself that the customers you are teaching to handle their own needs in the future will free up your time to work more with those who want you to take care of them.

- 7–11 points. You show no particular preference for customers who need quite a bit of help versus those who want you to teach them how to serve themselves. You will feel equally comfortable working with either of these types of people.

- 12–15 points. You show a preference for customers who know what they want and don't require a lot of attention. You are probably also most comfortable with customers who want you to show them how to use systems so they can serve themselves independently. You may be challenged by the customers who have no interest in helping themselves but want you to do things or make decisions for them. Consider explaining to the more dependent customer that you want to be helpful to

him or her and that you must serve others as well, so you don't have much time. Establish time limits if possible. Also remind yourself that this customer is a challenge for you and that serving this person's needs is your opportunity to enrich your own behavior.

4. *Preference for doing multiple tasks simultaneously.* While most customer service situations are fast paced and require multitasking, some allow more opportunities to complete one job at a time before moving to the next. This subscale measures the degree to which you are comfortable balancing multiple tasks simultaneously.

- 2–4 points. You indicate a preference for doing one task at a time. You will be most comfortable in customer service situations that allow you to focus on one customer's needs at a time. You will be most challenged by customer service situations where you are consistently being interrupted and asked to manage several customers simultaneously. For example, public desk areas that require you to attend to customers in line as well as those who persist in asking "a quick question" outside of the line, while also answering telephones, may be difficult for you. You are likely to most enjoy those times when customers are approaching you in a relatively slow though steady pace. If you are in a multitask situation, seek ways in which you can get short breaks from the public area. Volunteer for those behind-the-scenes jobs that most customer service areas require so that you can get some relief from the constant demands of multitasking.

- 5–7 points. You show no preference for focusing on one task versus managing multiple tasks simultaneously. You can adapt to whichever type of customer service environment you find yourself in.

- 8–10 points. You enjoy working on multiple items simultaneously and will enjoy customer service situations that allow you to work with more than one person or task at a time. You are likely to enjoy the busiest times of the day or year, when you need to serve several customers at a time. You are most likely to be challenged by situations or times that are less busy. During those times, you may wish to identify how you might help others or complete projects that will add value to the customer service of your organization.

5. *Preference for flexible rules.* While some customer service situations have very fixed rules that require (or allow) you to make virtually no decisions, others ask that you make decisions for each customer based on your best evaluation of the situation and the customer's needs. This subscale identifies the degree to which you prefer a fixed rule that treats every customer the same or flexibility that allows you to decide the best solution based on individual customer needs.

   - 2–4 points. You indicate a preference for fixed, predictable rules. You are likely to be uncomfortable with flexible rules that require you to make customer service decisions based on the situation. It may feel unfair to you. You are likely to prefer rules that are applied equally to each customer. Remember that no rule can cover every situation. As long as flexibility does not create undue hardship on other customers or the organization, try to think of each situation as unique. You will provide much more effective customer service by doing so.

   - 5–7 points. You have not shown a clear preference for flexible or fixed rules. You are likely to feel comfortable in settings with the flexibility that allows you to make situational decisions or with fixed rules that require you to handle each customer situation the same way.

   - 8–10 points. You indicate a preference for flexible rules that allow you to consider the situation and respond to each customer based on your assessment of what is best. You will be most challenged by rules that allow you no options to accommodate individual customer needs when you believe it would be good customer service to do so. If you are in a situation that does not allow for such flexibility, remind yourself that there may be a benefit to consistency. If you interpret the rules differently in

too many situations, you may create a customer service problem for another employee or create unequal customer treatment. You may consider acknowledging to customers that you would prefer a more flexible system but that you understand the need to be consistent in order to avoid unequal treatment of customers.

6. *Preference for working with people who are different from yourself.* Customer service work typically allows you to work with a wide range of people. Face-to-face work usually involves the greatest range of different encounters, with telephone contact providing other potential differences. This subscale asks you to consider how comfortable you are with people who may look different from you, communicate differently from you, or conduct business differently from you.

   - 3–6 points. You indicate you are most comfortable in working with people like yourself. The more different someone is from you, the more challenged you may be. Language or other differences that require you to struggle to understand the customer may be an irritant. Using empathy by asking yourself how you might feel if you were trying to get assistance from someone who could not understand you or who might get impatient with you might help you maintain patience and take the time necessary to leave these customers feeling well served.

   - 7–11 points. You have indicated no particular preference for working with people who are either similar to or different from you, and you will likely approach each customer with the same level of interest and service.

   - 12–15 points. You indicate a preference for working with people who are different from yourself. You may find these customers interesting and stimulating. Those people who are most like you may seem less engaging. You may benefit from watching the degree to which you show preference for those who are different from yourself, which could potentially result in less quality service to those most like you. Consider playing an anthropologist: when working with people who appear to be most like you, try to identify ways in which they are really not like you at all. This will not only make them more interesting to you but will also sharpen your observational skills.

7. *Preference for completing tasks*. Most customer service jobs require serving as many customers as possible. Balancing the completion of tasks (usually identified as the number of customers you serve) with developing effective relationships with customers so they will return to you is one of the greater challenges of customer service work. This subscale identifies the degree to which you prefer to complete tasks as quickly as possible versus spending time developing relationships with customers as you complete the task of serving them.

   • 2–4 points. You have indicated a greater preference for developing relationships with your customers than for just getting the job done. You are likely to prefer the customer who wants to talk for a bit before getting down to business. Customers who are not interested in visiting with you—if only briefly—may appear rude to you. Remind yourself when you have these customers that serving them as quickly as possible will make them happy and will allow you more time to develop a relationship with the next customer you meet.

   • 5–7 points. You have not indicated a clear preference for customers who want to visit a little to develop a relationship or those who want to get their business with you finished and leave as quickly as possible. You will easily serve each of these types of customers.

   • 8–10 points. You have indicated a greater preference for getting the job done than for visiting or developing relationships with customers. You will be most challenged by those customers who want to visit a little before they begin to conduct their business with you. You may be particularly comfortable in a faster-paced customer service setting that allows very little time to visit and requires that you keep moving on to the next customer. Remind yourself that people are your task. Identify a few

relationship-type statements or questions that can allow you to leave this customer feeling good while also getting the task done. For example, "I would enjoy having the time to visit with you, but I have three other telephone lines holding for me and I want to keep all of our customers happy. Please allow me to take your order as quickly as possible so I can be helpful to the others as well."

8. *Comfort level with conflict*. One of the most difficult challenges in customer service is serving the person who is dissatisfied or angry. The items in this subscale allow you to identify the degree to which you are comfortable handling conflict, helping the customer who is angry, or denying a customer's request.

   • 8–19 points. Your answers indicate that harmony is important to you. Customers' frustration or anger and conflict situations make you uncomfortable. You may have difficulty denying a customer request, even if it is unreasonable. You are also likely to be ill at ease with the customer who is demanding—even if you understand it is not about you. Be cautious about what you agree to do for a customer; you may run the risk of agreeing to something that violates good judgment, fairness, policy, or your own boundaries. Review such decisions with a co-worker who can help reinforce good decisions and provide you with feedback about other ways to handle uncomfortable situations.

   • 20–27 points. You have not indicated either a clear discomfort or comfort with conflict, frustration, or anger. A customer's negative feelings are generally not a source of discomfort for you. Although you may not be comfortable with the negativity, neither do you feel a need to avoid it; instead, you handle it when the situation requires.

   • 28–40 points. Your answers indicate that you are generally comfortable with conflict in customer service situations. You recognize that the customer's feelings are almost never about you, and you are able to hear and respond to his or her concerns in an effective manner. You are usually able to disagree with a customer and stand firm on regulations, even if the customer responds negatively. Try to be cautious about your disagreements, though. You may have a tendency to disagree more quickly than necessary, sometimes in situations where your ideas or opinions are not necessarily helpful. Ask yourself whether your behavior is really appropriate in this situation. Review these decisions with a co-worker who can provide feedback and reinforce your good decisions.

9. *Self-awareness and tolerance.* People providing customer service always bring their own attitudes and biases to the job, which affects how they respond to customers. The customer who is "difficult" for one person will not be for another. Understanding your own behavioral preferences is helpful so you can identify what type of customer situations are most likely to be troublesome for you. This allows you to watch for those situations and handle them more effectively.

   - 8–19 points. While you indicate a clear awareness of your own preferred behaviors and biases, customers whose behaviors you find offensive, or who are very different from you, may challenge you. Begin looking for two or three alternative ways to serve people whose behaviors you don't like. Look for positive explanations for such behaviors.

   - 20–27 points. Your customer service skills could probably be improved by taking time to reflect on your own attitudes and biases to identify areas where you might become more flexible. You might also have some difficulty identifying why you are challenged more by some customers than by others. Ask yourself after each "difficult" exchange why it was difficult for you. Focus on your own feelings, not on the customer's behaviors. Identify the behaviors you have most problems with and then look for a couple of alternative strategies for handling those types of customers when you are working with them.

   - 28–40 points. You have a high level of awareness regarding your own attitudes and biases. You work hard to empathize

with customers and to be flexible in meeting their needs. You are likely to be effective with most customer populations—or at least to be aware of which situations are challenging and that you may need to work on or, if possible, refer to others. You will generally have an easier time than others in serving customers who exhibit behaviors you don't care for.

10. *Comfort level with ambiguity and/or change.* Customer service work often involves changing situations, changing products, or changing customers. Such changes can often leave the people providing customer service with situations or people they don't understand and/or with the need to change how they are operating. This subscale looks at how comfortable you are with changes or situations that are unclear or new to you.

   - 3–6 points. You indicate a preference for predictability and may be more challenged by customers you cannot understand or by frequent changes in your work environment, including new technology. Remind yourself that those things you are comfortable with were new to you at one time. To the degree possible, limit the new things you are learning at one time. Ask co-workers to help you understand or identify ways to manage changing schedules and new issues, products, or people.

   - 7–11 points. You indicate no particular preference for change or stability, so these issues may not affect you.

   - 12–15 points. Your responses indicate comfort with change and flexibility. You may enjoy new types of customers, services, and technology. You may feel bored if your work becomes too routine or predictable. You may have a tendency to create changes because you like them. Be careful not to overwhelm your co-workers who are less comfortable with change than you are. You may also be a coach or mentor for those who are struggling with changes in procedures, customers, or technology.

11. *Preference for feedback.* Some customers provide considerable feedback (both positive and negative), some only give you feedback when they are satisfied, some only let you know

when they are unhappy, and some never provide any information about how your service has helped them. This subscale helps you look at your own preference for receiving feedback.

- 4–10 points. You indicate that you prefer to come to your own assessment of your performance and have no need to hear feedback from others. You may even feel annoyed by customers who give you "helpful suggestions" or positive acknowledgment, even though you believe they mean well. When someone provides you with feedback, simply say thank you and move on. You may also want to consider whether you are giving others feedback. If you don't need feedback, you may not be giving it, which may leave your customers feeling that you are not serving them well.
- 11–13 points. You indicate no clear preference for feedback and are likely to hear it if it is offered but not miss it when it is not.
- 14–20 points. You indicate that you enjoy getting feedback from others. Even negative feedback is welcomed because it allows you to know how others perceive your work and to improve. You may be more challenged by customers who never provide feedback; you have no idea whether you have met their needs. If you want more feedback from customers who don't usually provide it, consider asking them to give you information about whether you have been helpful. Be sure to ask this question in an open-ended manner. For example, "How else might I be helpful?"

12. *Preference for status and formality.* Some customers are from cultural backgrounds where they learn to be comfortable with status differentiation and formality. They are likely to address you (and wish to be addressed) by formal titles such as "Mrs.," "Mr.," or "Dr." They are also likely to expect problems to be solved by the individual with the highest status, such as a manager. They may also treat customer service employees as inferior in status. Other customers will be from cultural backgrounds that encourage informality and

equality. These individuals are likely to address everyone, and prefer to be addressed, by their first names. They will allow anyone to help them because the status of a manager is relatively meaningless to them. This subscale allows you to identify your own preference in the area of status and formality.

- 4–10 points. You indicate a preference for informality. You are likely to address others—and prefer to be addressed—by your first name. Customers who address you by title may appear distant, unfriendly, or cold to you. This can lead customers who prefer formality to experience you as inappropriately familiar or disrespectful. You are likely to have a strong preference for equality, so customers who expect you to serve them without common courtesies or respect (for example, saying "please" or "thank you") may seem rude to you. Customers who treat you as if they expect you to serve them are often from cultures where people have very specific role responsibilities, and the individual being served would never presume to become too familiar with or even acknowledge the server.
- 11–13 points. You show little preference for either formality or informality. You are not likely to be concerned with (or about) whether customers address you formally or informally. Nor are you likely to react to customers who demonstrate neither an expectation of nor appreciation for service.
- 14–20 points. You indicate a preference for greater formality as demonstrated by use of titles. You may feel the customer who uses—or even asks for—your first name is being disrespectful. You are also likely to address customers by their title, which may feel cold or distant to those who prefer informality. You may appreciate role differentiation and not be bothered by those customers who treat you as if they expect to be served and show little appreciation for your assistance. Customers who don't want to deal with you but who ask to see the manager or the person in charge don't upset you. Remind yourself that most people are acting in ways that

they feel are respectful and appropriate and that if the customer's preference is not the same as yours, it is not likely intended to be disrespectful. You might also listen to how the customer talks to you and match the level of informality.

Cultural Interactions

Time Required

70 minutes (10 minutes for individual work; 20 minutes for small-group work; 20 minutes for reporting and large-group discussion; 20 minutes for debriefing)

Objectives

1. To identify five important personal values
2. To identify five values important to your organization
3. To identify the effect on an individual when her or his values do or do not match those of the organization

Materials

- Personal/Work Values Worksheet for each participant
- Flipchart and marking pens
- Pens or pencils for participants

Process

1. Give participants the "Personal/Work Values" worksheet and ask them to circle the five values on the sheet that are *most important to them personally*. Also direct them to mark the five values that are perceived to be *most important to the organization* in which they work.
2. When they have finished with their marking, place them in groups of 3–5 people, asking that they identify the five values they believe to be most important to the organization in which they work. Give participants enough time to reach consensus.
3. Ask each small group to report to the large group the five values they have identified and to record these on a flipchart, noting any duplication.
4. Ask the large group to discuss first the impact on individuals of working in an organization whose primary values match their own and, second, the impact of working in an organization whose primary values do not match their individual primary values. What feelings arise and what behaviors might be exhibited?

   Note: Individuals are not asked to share their five most important personal values. If this is done, it will increase the risk of the activity to individuals.

Debriefing Questions

1. How easily did your small groups identify organizational values? On which of the following was it easiest to agree (a) identifying your personal values, (b) identifying organizational values and comparing them with your personal choices, (c) discussing the organizational values as a group and reaching a consensus, (d) trying to identify contrasting values, or (e) discussing values and cultural differences in the organization? Hardest?

2. How did you feel as you read through the values list? How did you feel about the alignment or lack of alignment between your personal values and the values of your organization?

3. What values were demonstrated during your small-group discussion? What behaviors were helpful to your participation? Were there any that interfered with your participation?

4. How did you reach a consensus?

5. What have you learned?

6. How could you apply what you have learned to your work life?

Debriefing Conclusions

1. Employees are generally able to agree about what workplace values are, based on their experiences in the organization.

2. Employees' perceptions of workplace values may not match any stated or written values of the organization.

3. Identifying personal values can help you understand areas where you are comfortable or uncomfortable in your work environment.

4. The closer personal values are aligned with the values of the organization, the more likely you are to experience a sense of significance about your work and/or a sense of job satisfaction. If personal and organizational values are not aligned, personal stress may result.

5. Identifying similarities and differences in values can help build an atmosphere where differences can be discussed and understanding can be built.

Adapted from an activity in *Understanding and Working with Values* by Brian P. Hall and Martin L. W. Hall.

Personal/Work Values Worksheet

Circle the five values most important to you personally. then put checks beside those values that you perceive to be most important to your organization.

1. **Collaboration**: cooperating with others to assign responsibilities and to complete projects

2. **Competition**: possessing a sense of rivalry—not only with others but with myself—to be first and most respected in a given area

3. **Creativity**: displaying original thought and expression that bring new ideas and images to the organization in concrete ways that did not previously exist

4. **Diversity**: believing that an organization is creatively enhanced by people from a variety of cultures and ethnic and educational backgrounds

5. **Economic Success**: attaining favorable financial results in business through effective control and management of resources

6. **Efficiency/Planning**: thinking about and designing projects in the best possible and least wasteful manner before implementing them

7. **Equality**: legal, social, and economic equality for all people, including myself

8. **Global Harmony**: conducting business in a way that creates understanding, interdependence, and peace among nations in the business arena

9. **Harmony**: maintaining a peaceful social environment by avoiding conflicts

10. **Hierarchy/Order**: ranking people and things methodically to establish standards of what is good and proper

11. **Honesty**: expressing my feelings and thoughts in a straightforward, objective manner

12. **Innovation**: contributing new ideas for positive changes in the organization

13. **Loyalty**: staying with personal relationships and work organization for the long haul, even when things might be tough; giving my absolute best at all times

14. **Productivity**: generating and completing tasks and achieving externally established goals and expectations

15. **Reason**: thinking logically and reasonably; exercising reason before emotions

16. **Rules/Accountability**: having clear, written rules and holding everyone accountable to them

17. **Service**: contributing to the organization and society through my skills or knowledge

18. **Synergy**: experiencing the relationships of persons within the group to be harmonious and energized so that the achievements of the group far surpass the achievement of any individual

19. **Technology/Science**: use of all technological advances that can enhance my job

20. **Tradition**: ritualizing history and traditions as important links from the past to the future as a way to remember what we stand for

Adapted from an activity in *Understanding and Working with Values* by Brian P. Hall and Martin L. W. Hall.

36

What Is of Value?

Time Required

15–30 minutes (Use as an opener. Time depends on group size; conduct the debriefing later in the day.)

Objectives

1. To involve the participants in the design and direction of their learning
2. To provide the facilitator information on group chemistry and expectations
3. To provide objective data that can be examined relative to terminal and instrumental values

Materials

- 3 x 5 index cards
- Flipchart and marking pens (optional)

Process

1. After initially greeting the group, acknowledge that individuals have come to this training with their own set of expectations. As the facilitator, it is your desire to provide the best training session/ workshop possible and to meet both individual and group needs. To better understand their individual and group preferences, you will need their help.
2. Distribute a 3 x 5 index card to every participant.
3. Write on a flipchart or ask participants directly, "What is one thing that you personally hope to learn from this workshop? You will have two minutes to think about this and to write your response on this card."

   Note: Here are two alternative questions that might be used:
   "What is one question you hope to have answered today?"
   "What is one major concern or anxiety you have about this workshop?"

4. At the end of two minutes, ask participants to stand up and find a partner. Each pair will read both cards. As a team, they now have two minutes to choose one card or to combine the ideas in a way

that meets both partners' needs. At the end of two minutes, the pair moves on to find another pair. The 4 team members read both cards. They again have two minutes to decide which of the two cards they can agree on or to combine the ideas to meet everyone's needs. *(Note: At this time, with a group of 32, you will have 8 group expectations.)*

5. Then ask each group of 4 to share and post their card. Combine similar cards into one. Now review all of the expectations with the group and commit to meeting them to the best of your ability. If there is any posted expectation that you know you will not be able to address during the session, share that with the participants at this time to avoid unmet expectations at the end of the day.

Note: This activity provides an opportunity to observe group dynamics as well as gather information on group expectations. It involves people early in the day, forcing them to think about their responsibilities for identifying/achieving their own needs. Take care about how you introduce the combining/eliminating of expectations so that individuals aren't left feeling like their expectations or ideas were not valued if they were eliminated.

Debriefing Questions

Note: This activity is not debriefed until later in the day when you actually conduct a values module, lecture, or discussion. Remind people of this early activity and review the group cards that remained at the end of the activity.

1. What kinds of behaviors were used to decide which card(s) to keep or discard? Did you use cooperation or competition strategies? Direct or indirect communication? Relationship or task approaches?
2. How did you feel during this activity? Why?
3. What values were represented in the behaviors used to make decisions? What values are represented in the posted cards?
4. What have you learned?
5. How can you apply the learning from this activity to your daily work?

Debriefing Conclusion

Values form the foundation of our behaviors, our decisions, and our perceptions, even in an activity as "simple" as identifying expectations for a workshop.

Adapted from an activity presented by Sivasailam Thiagarajan at The Summer Institute for Intercultural Communication, 2000.

37

Four Case Studies

<table>
<tr><td>Work</td></tr>
<tr><td>M–H</td></tr>
<tr><td>P, T, O, D, M</td></tr>
</table>

Time Required

50 minutes (15 minutes for individual responses to case studies; 20 minutes for small-group discussion; 15 minutes for debriefing)

Objectives

1. To provide participants with an opportunity to explore personal values
2. To generate discussion about cultural influence on values
3. To explore differences in perspective regarding values

Materials

- Copies of the Four Case Studies handout for each participant
- Transparency of Four Case Studies: Discussion Questions
- Projector or flipchart and marking pen for questions

Process

1. Pass out copies of the "Four Case Studies" handout to all of the participants.
2. Allow 10–15 minutes for participants to read and select responses to the four case studies. Participants are to make two choices for each case study: one for themselves personally and one that they believe "others in your organization" would select.
3. Form groups of 3–6 people and ask participants to share their responses in their groups, using the questions below for each case study. Allow approximately 20 minutes for this discussion.

   Note: The questions should be placed on an overhead transparency (see transparency master on page 149) or flipchart for easy viewing by the entire group. Remind participants that there are no right or wrong answers and that this is an opportunity to identify differences and possible reasons for those differences. Also remind them that this is an opportunity to listen to each other—to learn, not to persuade.

   - Which choice did individuals on your team make most frequently?
   - If some of you made different choices from the group, why do you think this was so?

- What are some of the important values or beliefs that are reflected by your choices?
- How closely aligned were personal choices with organizational choices?
- What are the implications for those responses in which personal and organizational choices differ?

Debriefing Questions

1. Which cases were easiest to agree on? Why? Hardest? Why?
2. How did you feel during the discussion—especially if your responses were different from those of the majority of the group?
3. What values were you able to identify as affecting responses?
4. What have you learned?
5. How can you apply what you learned to your everyday work life?

Debriefing Conclusions

1. Our values can be challenged when we have to make difficult decisions.
2. Our values do affect our decisions.
3. When our personal and organizational values are not aligned, the results can create discomfort.
4. When our values are different from the majority, we can either feel like an outsider (marginalized) or feel "righteous" (superior) about our own value position.
5. When either terminal (the goal) values or instrumental (the behavior used to get to the goal) values differ between two people, the result can be misperceptions or conflict if we don't explore the differences and listen carefully.

Four Case Studies: Discussion Questions

- Which choice did individuals on your team pick most frequently?

- Identify the reasons of those who made other choices.

- What are some of the important values or beliefs that are reflected by your choices?

- How aligned were personal choices with organizational choices?

- What are the implications for those responses in which personal and organizational choices differ?

Four Case Studies Handout

For each study, choose one response for yourself and one response that you think others in your organization would select.

1. You are appointed to head a new work team on a project that is critical to the organization. This is your first important leadership role, and you are preparing for your first team meeting. Based on your personal ideas about team building, which statement is the best reflection of your thinking?
   a. I will guide the team by helping members solve problems, but I will have the final word on all decisions because I am ultimately responsible.
   b. I will take charge early. My role is to maintain balance between setting goals and ensuring that the goals are met.
   c. My first responsibility will be to develop a relationship with each team member. Team members will also need time to learn about each other to facilitate strong commitment and stellar performance.
   d. I will provide all of the information about the project, including information about deadlines, expectations, budget, and so on. I will also find ways to engage team members so they can make a clear commitment to the project
   e. I will need to pay close attention to performance, task completion, and goal achievement—I will reward each member for what she or he contributes to the project—anything else is irrelevant.

   Your choice_____

   Others in your organization would choose_____

2. You are the contractor remodeling a home for a friend. The work crew has informed you that you will be a month behind the promised completion date because the job is complicated and your original completion, date was unrealistic. Your friends have already mailed invitations to a wedding and reception in their newly remodeled home based on the original completion date. What would you do?

   a. I will pay the crew whatever is necessary to complete the job by the promised time. This customer is my personal friend to whom I have made a promise, so the job must be completed on time.
   b. My first obligation is to my employees. The delay is due to my unrealistic schedule, not because the crew is not working hard enough. I need to tell my friend that we will not be able to finish by the date promised.
   c. I am responsible for promising an unrealistic completion date, and it would be unfair to ask my crew to work overtime. I will offer financial compensation to my friend for the cost involved in moving the wedding date or location.
   d. Business is business. I promised the completion date based on the available information. It may be inconvenient for my friend, but she should understand and modify her plans.
   e. I will tell my friends that the work crew is inexperienced and the unexpected delay is their fault.

   Your choice_____

   Others in your organization would choose_____

3. You are riding in a car with a friend. He turns to say something to you, loses concentration, and hits a car parked at the curb. In addition to being distracted by your conversation, he was also driving well over the speed limit. He asks you to testify in court that he was driving the speed limit, which will save him from damaging his driving record and from an even larger increase in his insurance rates. There are no other witnesses. How would you act in this case?
   a. I am under obligation to tell the truth under oath. I will not perjure myself. A real friend would not ask me to lie.

b. I will not lie under oath, but I will offer my friend emotional and financial support if he needs it.

c. My friend has my full support. Courts and laws are often irrelevant to real-life situations.

d. My friend is my main concern, but I will encourage him to tell the truth.

e. I will testify that I was not able to see the speedometer but think we may have been speeding a little.

Your choice_____

Others in your organization would choose_____

4. Gender issues have been an area of increasing concern for organizations around the world. As you are walking through the manufacturing plant, you hear each of the following statements. Which one most clearly expresses your thoughts?

a. For women to contribute to an organization where physical demands are part of the job, they need special consideration and accommodation. The organization must make the necessary adjustments so women receive the opportunities they deserve in order to succeed.

b. Equality means exactly that. Treating women differently from men is not fair. Women should be treated and evaluated with the same standards as men.

c. Women have different talents and perspectives than men. Equal means they have an opportunity to share their diverse viewpoints and to contribute their unique talents.

d. If women fight for positions in a "man's world," they may lose the unique talents that they bring. If they lead in a male style, the result will be business as usual. It is important to provide alternative ways for women to enter leadership roles.

e. If things are to be equal, the focus should be on talent and performance, not gender.

Your choice_____

Others in your organization would choose_____

38

Discovering Team Strengths and Values

Adaptable

M–H

P, T, D, M

Time Required

100 minutes (15 minutes to prepare personal stories; 45 minutes in triads; 10 minutes to record skills and values on flipchart; 30 minutes for large-group reports and debriefing)

Objectives

1. To use personal stories to help team members learn about strengths and values of other team members
2. To facilitate the formation of a positive foundation for team member relationships
3. To identify "best practices" within the team

Materials

- Paper and pencils
- Flipchart and marking pens

Process

1. Introduce the activity by telling participants that they will all share stories that reflect their personal and professional strengths and core values. Core values may be explicit or implicit within the story.
2. Ask participants to take a few minutes to think of several experiences from their personal or professional life where they felt particularly good about both the event and their own role in it. Ask them to select one of those events and prepare to tell others a story about it. The story should include as much detail as possible and should specifically address the following questions:
   - What was the general purpose of the event?
   - Were there obstacles you needed to overcome?
   - What motivated you to invest your energy and time in this event?
   - How were you able to accomplish your goal?
   - Were there surprises along the way?
   - What did you learn about yourself? About others?
   - How did you feel at the time? How do you feel now?
   - How has this experience influenced your belief about yourself/ your abilities?

3. Place participants in groups of three. Tell the groups they will have 45 minutes, during which time each individual is to tell his or her story and receive feedback from the group. Remind groups to manage their time so that no individual dominates.

   Note: If there is a mix of older and newer members on the team, be sure to have a mix of new and old members in each of the small groups.

4. Tell the groups that as they are listening to each speaker, they are to make two lists: (1) skills or talents they hear the individual describing during the story being shared and (2) values they hear the storyteller revealing, either implicitly or explicitly. Listeners will then review their lists and identify three skills and three core values they heard reflected in the story. Each listener will share their three strengths and three values with the storyteller. Make it clear that every listener is to share his or her list *even if it repeats others;* these repetitions are expected. It is important for the speaker to hear from each group member. After listeners have shared, the speaker is given an opportunity to respond to the feedback by answering these questions:
   • Do you agree with the skills identified?
   • How do you feel those skills are utilized in this work team?
   • Do you agree with the values identified?
   • How do you feel those values are acknowledged in the work team?

   Each group member follows this pattern until all members have had the opportunity to share their story with the others.

5. While the groups are telling their stories, prepare two newsprint sheets for team members to record their compilation of skills and values. Label one sheet "Skills" and the other, "Values."

6. Next, ask the small groups to identify all of the skills and values from their three stories. Ask the group to select one member from each small group to record their collection of skills and values on the newsprint sheets.

7. Reconvene the larger group and examine the lists of skills and values, then have the participants answer the following questions:
   • Given this information about our skills and values, what conclusions can we draw about our team's best practices? That is, how can we maximize the use of our skills and values?
   • Which of these listed skills are a good match with the responsibilities of our team?
   • Are there skills we need that we don't have enough of? If so, how might we obtain them?
   • Are there skills that we have an abundance of? If so, how can we avoid competing to use those skills?
   • Do we share many values, according to this list? How could this impact our team work?
   • If there are inconsistent or competing values, how can we operate to allow both values to exist?
   • Are there values listed that could be detrimental to the team's performance? If so, how might we manage that?

Debriefing Questions

1. How did you feel initially when you heard about the activity? How did you feel as the small group was forming?
2. How did you feel when you found out you had to choose an event and share it?
3. How do you feel now that the activity has been completed? What values did you see demonstrated by other group members as they participated?
4. Which actions or behaviors were helpful to you as you worked with the small group? Were there actions or behaviors that interfered with your group participation?
5. Which of your own values apply to this situation?
6. What have you learned from your experience today?
7. How could you apply information from this experience to your work life?

Debriefing Conclusions

1. Individuals bring their strengths and values to the group and to their organizations.
2. Sharing personal stories (and strengths and values) can enhance our understanding of one another and our working relationships.
3. Participants are better able to remember others' core strengths through the shared stories.
4. Reflective feedback reinforces core strengths and fosters collegial relationships.
5. Information about strengths and values can be used to strengthen team processes.

Adapted from Dr. Kristine Sullivan's presentation on Dr. Bernard Haldane's Dependable Strengths Process, Seattle University, Seattle, Washington, 1999.

39

Your Values Meet the Team's Values

Time Required

70–80 minutes (10 minutes for introductory lecturette; 10 minutes for self-assessment; 10 minutes to mark overhead; 20 minutes for small-group work; 20–30 minutes for debriefing)

Objectives

1. To identify values of individual team members
2. To establish the values profile of the team
3. To determine values that create opportunities for and barriers to team effectiveness
4. To identify ways to eliminate barriers to and maximize opportunities for team effectiveness

Materials

- A Values Continuum Worksheet for each person
- A Values Continuum Worksheet transparency or newsprint
- An overhead projector (or a flipchart) and several colored projector pens (or sticky dots) for identifying team values

Process

1. Open the session with a brief lecturette regarding culture and values (see "Culture and Values Narrative," Appendix A, page 231).
2. Give all of the participants the "Values Continuum" worksheet and ask them to complete it for themselves.
3. Ask each team member to mark his or her individual value choices on the "Values Continuum" worksheet transparency or to use sticky dots to identify his or her choices on the easel page. This will create a team profile that everyone can see.
4. Place people in groups of 3–4 and ask them to discuss where the team's opportunities and challenges may lie, based on the group profile. Ask them to pay particular attention to values where the grouping is tight as well as to values where there may be individuals whose values differ from the majority.
5. Bring the groups together and ask them to report the opportunities and challenges they have identified.

6. In the large group, try to agree on specific behaviors that will help the team maximize their opportunities and reduce or eliminate the barriers to effectiveness.
7. Ask the team to commit to practicing at least two of the behaviors to maximize effectiveness and two behaviors to minimize barriers.

Debriefing Questions

1. Which values resulted in the greatest spread across the continuum? Why do you think this is so? Which value resulted in the highest degree of agreement? Why?
2. How did you feel when one of your values differed markedly from the team's?
3. How did you feel about the discussions?
4. Was it easy or difficult to identify opportunities and challenges? In what ways?
5. What have you learned?
6. How will you apply what you learned to your everyday work life?

Debriefing Conclusions

1. When the team is in close agreement on a value, it can be a strength and facilitate effectiveness—or it can create blind spots the team needs to be aware of.
2. When an individual differs from the majority of the team on a value, that person can be a strength to the team if he or she is not made an outsider.

Values Continuum Worksheet

Circle the number (between 1 and 7) that most closely represents your value. For example, if you are *very* formal, circle number 1; if you are *very* informal, circle number 7; if you have no preference for formality or informality, circle number 4, and so on.

1.	Formal	1	2	3	4	5	6	7	Informal
2.	Listening	1	2	3	4	5	6	7	Talking
3.	Structured	1	2	3	4	5	6	7	Flexible
4.	Tradition	1	2	3	4	5	6	7	Change
5.	Collaboration	1	2	3	4	5	6	7	Competition
6.	What you know	1	2	3	4	5	6	7	Who you know
7.	Task	1	2	3	4	5	6	7	Relationship
8.	Fixed rules	1	2	3	4	5	6	7	No rules
9.	Harmony (by avoiding issues)	1	2	3	4	5	6	7	Harmony (by confronting issues)
10.	Customer first	1	2	3	4	5	6	7	Company first
11.	Team	1	2	3	4	5	6	7	Individual
12.	Security	1	2	3	4	5	6	7	Risk
13.	Hierarchy	1	2	3	4	5	6	7	Equity
14.	Quality	1	2	3	4	5	6	7	Quantity
15.	Long-term goals	1	2	3	4	5	6	7	Short-term goals

40

Simulation: Rockets and Sparklers

Time Required

90 minutes (15 minutes to learn cultural rules; 10 minutes for visits and small-group debriefing; 15 minutes to play together; 15 minutes to describe the other culture; 35 minutes for large-group sharing and debriefing)

Objectives

1. To identify the different aspects of culture: values and behaviors
2. To explore the influence of culture on our interpretation of others' behaviors
3. To demonstrate the influence of cultural values on our own behaviors

Materials

- Copies of the Sparklers' Cultural Rules Handout and the Rockets' Cultural Rules Handout for each member of the assigned cultures
- Paper clips
- A breakout room for one of the cultures

Process

1. This activity offers participants firsthand experience with a "cultural encounter." After dividing the group in half, distribute the "Sparklers' Cultural Rules" handout to each member of one group and the "Rockets' Cultural Rules" handout to each participant in the other group. Give each group approximately 10 minutes to read over the characteristics of their culture and to practice the "Paper Clip Game," using their cultural rules to do so. Except for the scouts, groups should continue to play the game.
2. Ask each group to send 2 or 3 scouts into the other culture to observe their interactions. They are not to participate in the culture; they should only observe. These scouts spend approximately five minutes in the other culture. Upon returning to their home culture, they share what they have seen and describe what they believe to be the rules and values of the other culture.

3. After the scouts have briefed their own cultural group on the other culture, ask both cultural groups to meet in the same room and give them approximately 15 minutes to play the "Paper Clip Game" together.

4. After 15 minutes, separate the two groups again and give each culture 15 minutes with their group to prepare a description of the other culture, which they will be asked to share once they are together again. Specifically, each group is to respond to the following questions:

   • What behaviors did your scouts observe? What cultural values or rules did your scouts determine from these observations?

   • When you were first together as a total group and playing the game, what observations did you make? How accurate did you feel the scouts had been in describing what they saw? Were there differences in what the scouts described and your own experience?

   • Using descriptive words, how would you portray the other culture?

5. After 15 minutes, bring the two groups together again. Ask the Sparklers to share their descriptions of the Rockets' culture with the Rockets. Do not allow the Rockets to talk during this time—they are only to listen. When the Sparklers are finished, allow the Rockets to share their conclusions about the Sparklers. Do not allow the Sparklers to talk during this time—they are only to listen.

Debriefing Questions

1. How similar or different was each culture from the assumptions the other culture made about them? What might arise from these perceptions? *(Note: Look for both resources each might bring and conflicts that might occur.)*

2. How did you feel about being in your own "culture"? Why? If you were a scout, how did you feel about the behaviors of the other culture when you played in the large group? Why?

3. What personal values do you hold that made either of these cultures comfortable or uncomfortable?

4. Did you agree with the other culture's description of you? If not, what was your reaction?

5. What did you learn from this experience?

6. How can you apply what you learned to everyday life? Are there groups in your organization that might misperceive each other in the way the Sparklers and Rockets did? Why?

Debriefing Conclusions

1. We perceive and evaluate others from our own cultural perspective.

2. We tend to interpret or evaluate others' behaviors rather than describing them—and the interpretation/evaluation is from our own cultural perspective. This can interfere with our ability to learn about another culture.

3. Individuals within a culture may interpret cultural rules differently, leading to individual differences in behaviors.
4. If we are too rigid (stereotyping) in our expectations of another culture, we may miss individual differences and be less effective in our interactions with individuals from that culture.
5. Our personal values may lead us to be more or less comfortable with the behavior of others.

Sparklers' Cultural Rules Handout

The most important goal or purpose in life for a Sparkler is the accumulation of wealth (paper clips). All members of the Sparkler culture receive an equal number of paper clips at birth and have an equal opportunity to accumulate more.

Individuals spend a great deal of time counting their paper clips. Really wealthy Sparklers display their paper clips by wearing them as jewelry or attaching them to their clothing. The Sparklers with the greatest number of paper clips are the most highly respected in Sparkler society. Sparklers do not spend much time together unless they are engaged in the exchange of paper clips. They like to keep a "safe" distance of approximately two to three feet during paper clip exchanges, and they are not comfortable with people who stand too close. It is important to Sparklers to maintain eye contact during the game.

Paper Clip Game

In this culture it is important to be the initiator of the game. The initiator hides paper clips in either the right or left hand. If the other person guesses which hand holds the paper clips, he or she receives the paper clips that were in the hand. If the person guesses incorrectly, a paper clip is given to the initiator. Accumulating clips is important, so use your time in the most productive way. It is important to keep on the move and make a lot of contacts.

You discover that there is another culture not too far away that plays the paper clip game. This could be a great opportunity to accumulate more paper clips. Practice being a Sparkler for five minutes. Once you are comfortable being a Sparkler, you are then ready to send two or three Sparklers out to meet your neighbors, the Rockets. When the "scouts" return, they will report on their experience with this other culture. All of the Sparklers then can go to visit the Rockets and play the paper clip game.

Rockets' Cultural Rules Handout

Rockets love to be together. They love to laugh, talk, and tell stories. The thing most valued in this culture is relationships. Rockets can usually be found in groups of three or four. They touch each other on the shoulder or back as a form of greeting and ask about family members and each other's health. They rarely maintain eye contact for any length of time, and their eyes are always looking around.

Accumulating wealth is not highly valued; in fact, displaying wealth is not appropriate. Rockets are never greedy or pushy, and they don't care about winning games. Age is an important criterion for respect and authority. The oldest community member is the ruler, and when the ruler plays the game, he or she always wins.

Paper Clip Game

To play the paper clip game, a player hides a paper clip in either the right or left hand. The other player must guess which hand has the paper clip. If the person guesses correctly, he or she gets the clip. If wrong, he or she gives the other person a clip. Rockets should never act greedy or pushy. Remember, winning is not important.

Talking about family and telling stories is an important part of the game. Players exchange pleasantries before and after each exchange of paper clips. If the ruler approaches the group, everyone stops talking. Only after the ruler gives permission can the interaction continue. The ruler's role is to protect his or her people. Visitors are expected to behave like local people. If a visitor is breaking the cultural rules, that person must be ignored or exiled (asked to leave the room).

41

A Good Employee Is or Does

Time Required

85–95 minutes (10 minutes for introduction; 10 minutes for individual work; 30 minutes in small groups; 20–30 minutes for group reporting and discussion; 15 minutes for debriefing)

Objectives

1. To illustrate the ways that values influence our behavior
2. To examine the differences between visible and invisible cultural norms
3. To identify an organization's culture
4. To identify how organizational behavior is affected by dominant cultural values

Materials

- Paper and pencil
- Flipchart and marking pens
- Overhead projector
- Transparency of the Top Ten American Values sheet

Process

1. Introduce the concept of visible and invisible rules in organizations. Visible rules are verbal and/or written and are stated as rules, policies, procedures, or values. Invisible rules are unspoken and unwritten but important. Insiders (members) know these rules, either consciously or unconsciously.

2. Ask participants to individually answer the following question: *A good employee in this organization is or does what?* Caution participants to focus on invisible rules, not written policies and procedures. Give them approximately 10 minutes to individually identify the characteristics of a good employee, *or* give this as a homework assignment the day before the training.

   Note: Participants may ask if their answers are to be from management's perspective or from that of co-workers. Because managers usually develop the organization's culture by what they reward, have participants assume the point of view of management.

3. In groups of 4–5, ask participants to share their answers and try to reach group consensus on the four most important characteristics or behaviors for being perceived as a good employee in their organization. Allow approximately 30 minutes for this discussion.

4. Ask each group to share their top four items, recording them on newsprint so everyone can see them. Place a check next to any item that is duplicated by another group, rather than rewriting the item.

   Note: The most important invisible organizational rules will likely have several checks because everyone knows how important they are.

5. Ask the entire group to identify any rules that they *don't* think should be on the list. This will rarely happen, but occasionally there is something unique that surfaces in one small group that, upon discussion, isn't universally valued by the organization and should be removed from the list.

6. Point out to the group that organizational cultures form in the context of a larger national culture. The organizational culture has been developed by its members and leaders over the history of the organization and includes both written and unwritten, visible and invisible rules. Place the "Ten Top American Values" transparency (see transparency master on page 170) on an overhead projector. Now go through the list of invisible rules generated by the group and ask, for each item, if it supports one of the U.S. values. For example, many groups will say their organization values the employee who consistently shows up early, works hard, and stays late. That organizational value may be seen as supporting these U.S. values: work ethic, competition and winning, and doing and achieving.

7. If there are invisible rules that do not fit into any of the top ten U.S. cultural values, explore why that rule might be important in this particular organization.

8. At the end of this "comparison" process, identify how many of the U.S. values show up within this organization's rules and procedures (values).

Debriefing Questions

1. What part of this activity was easiest? Most difficult?
2. Do you have any personal values that might be in conflict with those of the organization? Might this conflict help explain areas of your work that are uncomfortable for you? What options do you have in managing those value conflicts?
3. What have you learned? If there are invisible rules that employees are being judged by, what can you do to help newer employees adjust to the organization's culture more quickly?
4. How can you apply what you have learned to your everyday work life?

Debriefing Conclusions

1. Our organizational behavior tends to be consistent with the dominant national cultural values.

2. Some of our behaviors or values at work may be different if the organizational purpose, mission, or operations fall outside the key dominant national cultural values.

3. We can make choices about which values and associated behaviors we embrace as an organization, but such choices require a conscious, ongoing process.

4. Employees who are culturally different from the organizational culture may have difficulty recognizing the invisible rules. As a result, these employees may be labeled as not "fitting in." The more we can translate those values into written rules or verbalize them to new employees, the more quickly each person can succeed in the organization.

5. Valuing diversity (and desiring to fully use the resources that diversity offers) leads us to examine organizational culture and to eliminate invisible rules that may be barriers to employee success.

6. Organizations that value diversity try to make rules visible by putting them in writing and/or stating them verbally.

7. The same values may drive very different behaviors. Sharing both the value and the expected behavior will lead to clearer understanding and success for most employees.

Optional Process

For use with managers or executives:

1. After obtaining the participants' list of characteristics and behaviors valued by the organization, ask the group to identify the business purpose each item serves.

2. For each item listed, ask the group to identify whether there is any group of individuals within the organization who might be excluded from full participation by any rule identified (and its underlying value). For example, if one of the organization's unwritten rules is people being at the office long hours ("face time"—being seen by insiders early in the morning and late at night), single parents or individuals with elderly parents or other family obligations will be at a distinct disadvantage. That same individual may be working just as many hours but may do so at home in the evenings. For each item where a potential detrimental effect is identified, ask the group to consider (a) alternative ways of achieving the same business goals and (b) a method for changing the informal rules to be more inclusive.

   Note: The above two steps can also be done with employees but only if management has indicated an interest in hearing ideas from employees and has a commitment to consider implementation of some of the ideas. If management has not indicated such interest and commitment, asking employees to engage in this process would only result in their dissatisfaction.

© Executive Diversity Services, Inc., Seattle, Washington, 1996.

Top Ten American Values

Individualism

Competition and Winning

Material Possessions and Comfort

Work Ethic

Doing and Achieving

Cooperation and Fair Play

Youth and Attractiveness

Progress/Change

Equality

Family

Sources (see Resource Bibliography for complete citations)
Gary Althen, *American Ways: A Guide for Foreigners in the United States.* 2d ed.
Edward C. Stewart and Milton J. Bennett, *American Cultural Patterns: A Cross-Cultural Perspective.* Rev. ed.

42

My Values

Adaptable
M–H
P, T, D, M

Time Required
60 minutes (5 minutes for individual work; 20 minutes for small-group discussion; 35 minutes for large-group discussion)

Objectives
1. To begin identifying personal values
2. To examine how differences in personal values can create conflict

Materials
- What I Value Handout
- Pens or pencils

Process
1. Have the participants complete the "What I Value" handout by choosing their top five values.
2. In small groups of 5–7 members, ask participants to share their responses. Focus on those choices that were different. How might these differences create conflict in the workplace?
3. Ask each group to identify one difference and share the workplace implications with the large group.

Debriefing Conclusions
1. We bring our personal values to work, and they determine our behavior and our perception of others' behavior.
2. Differing values may be a resource for us and also a likely source of conflict that we do not understand.
3. When we have conflicts in values, they are rarely identified as such. If two people differ in appearance (color, gender, ethnicity, disability, etc.), the conflict is often attributed to that difference. If there is no visible difference, the conflict is usually attributed to "personality differences." It is much easier to resolve conflicts when the source of the conflict has been accurately identified.

What I Value Handout

Please select the *five values* that are *most important* to you.

Accomplishment: To achieve something noteworthy; to experience satisfaction when I accomplish a task, or solve a problem

Aesthetic pleasure/beauty/art: To enjoy and respect things (e.g., music, art, nature, theater) that are aesthetically appealing and from which I derive pleasure

Being loved: To experience feelings of warmth, affection, and caring from others

Challenge: To participate in activities that engage my intellect and creativity

Creativity: To display original thoughts; to develop new ideas, solutions, and improvements, then implement them

Dedication: To be loyal to my family, organization, and social or political groups

Ethical standards: To maintain a sense of right and wrong; to hold to my personal or religious ideals

Faith: To have faith in my abilities and skills; to feel secure in the help of others and to recognize help and acknowledge help received

Friendship: To have a group with whom I can share ideas and experiences

Good times/pleasure: To have fun and enjoy myself

Growth: To expand my life through my job or work in the community; to increase my knowledge or skills; to find fulfillment where I work and live

Health (physical/mental): To maintain a sound mind and body; to feel energetic and free from pain; to feel free from worry and anxiety; to have peace of mind

Helpfulness: To be responsive and generous; to have empathy toward others; to provide assistance, support, or protection to others

Independence: To think and act without being subjected to outside constraints; to achieve my goals in a manner best suited to me; to have the freedom to come and go; to be true to myself at all times

Justice and parity: To help correct conditions of human oppression; to actualize the truth that all human beings are equal; to make contributions that help eliminate unjust treatment of others

Knowledge: To pursue truth; to learn new things and explore ideas; to feel intelligent and be known as an intelligent person

Love: To experience warmth, feelings of affection, caring, attachment to and interest in something or someone

Money: To be comfortable materially and to have sufficient income and assets

Power: To lead and direct others; to influence or control others to do what I want/believe needs to be done

Recognition: To receive attention, notice, and approval from others because of something I have done

Responsibility: To be personally accountable to others for a job or commitment; to own something and take care of it

Security: To have a safe place or relationship where I experience protection; to feel safe; to have self-confidence, job security, and income

Self-Esteem: To be someone of value in my own eyes and in the eyes of others; to feel useful and wanted; to be appreciated by others; to have those who know me confirm I am worthy of respect

Wisdom: To pursue ultimate truth and knowledge of objective and subjective realities; to understand the meaning of life

Adapted from exercises used by Executive Diversity Services, Inc., Seattle, Washington, 2002.

43

What Do They Bring?

Work

M–H

T, D

Time Required

70–90 minutes depending on the size and diversity of the team (5 minutes for introduction of topic; 15 minutes for small-group work; 30–50 minutes for large-group sharing and discussion; 20 minutes for debriefing)

Objectives

1. To identify the forms of diversity in a work group
2. To identify the value of the diversity that individuals bring to the group

Materials

- The Four Circles of Diversity Handout
- Flipchart and marking pens

Process

1. Using the broad definition of diversity in "The Four Circles of Diversity" handout, review the many characteristics, both visible and invisible, that individuals can bring to a work team.
2. Invite participants to form groups of 4–5 and then to identify the diversity available to them, listing all of the characteristics on easel paper.
3. Reconvene the larger group and have each small group share its list, identifying those characteristics the entire group shares.
4. Lead the group in a discussion of which characteristics do and do not matter to the group. For example, while there may be religious diversity in the group, it may not affect the way the group works together to achieve its goals. On the other hand, religious diversity could have meaning to the group if some individuals need prayer time during the day or take religious holidays different from the others.
5. After identifying the characteristics that do affect the group, discuss the advantages each of those characteristics can provide the group and the potential conflicts they may create within the group.
6. Have the group identify specific strategies for maximizing the strengths and minimizing the conflicts of those characteristics they have identified.

7. Ask the group to develop a written agreement listing their behavioral objectives for maximizing the strengths and minimizing the conflicts of their diverse characteristics.

Debriefing Questions

1. What happened during the small-group and large-group discussions? Who talked most/least? Why?
2. How did you feel during the discussions? Were you able to fully express your ideas? Why or why not? Were there conflicts or disagreements?
3. What personal values affected your responses to this discussion?
4. What have you learned?
5. How can you apply what you learned to the work team?

Debriefing Conclusions

1. All groups contain visible and invisible differences.
2. If members feel like "outsiders" because of some diverse characteristic they bring to the team, they may feel less able to participate fully in the group's work.
3. It is sometimes easier to identify the conflicts created by diversity than to identify the resources it provides.
4. Some differences matter to a work team; others do not, although they may be very important to the individuals who possess those differences.

Adapted from an activity by Donna Goldstein in *Experiential Activities for Intercultural Learning,* edited by H. Ned Seelye.

The Four Circles of Diversity Handout

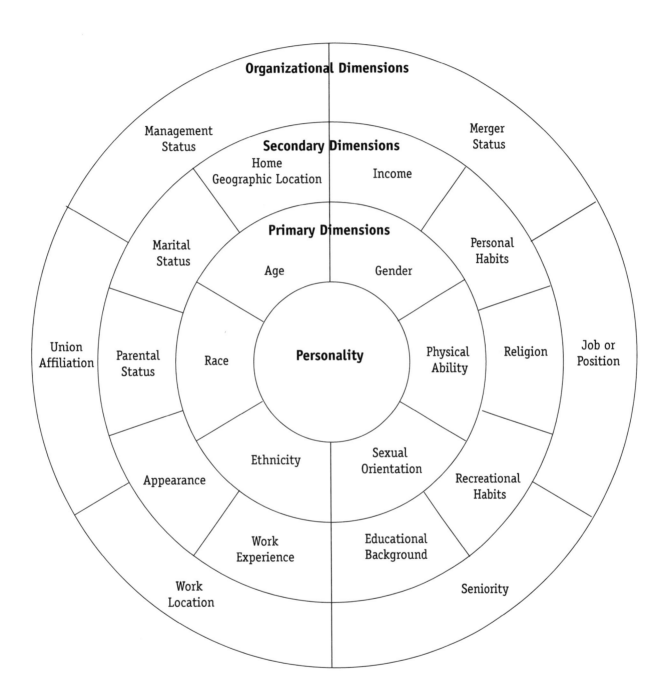

Adapted from a figure in *Diverse Teams at Work: Capitalizing on the Power of Diversity*, by Lee Gardenswartz and Anita Rowe.

44

Behaviors I Find Difficult

Work

M–H

P, D, M

Time Required

90 minutes (10 minutes for lecturette; 10 minutes for individual work; 30 minutes for small-group discussion; 20 minutes for large-group sharing and discussion; 20 minutes for debriefing)

Objectives

1. To identify behaviors participants find difficult
2. To identify the potential values sources of those behaviors
3. To identify whether the behavior matters in the workplace
4. To identify ways to address such behaviors

Materials

- Differences in Cultural Values Worksheet (see Appendix B, page 233)
- Values Differences Handout (see Appendix C, page 235)

Process

1. Give a lecturette on cultural values differences and on whether the "difference makes a difference" (see the "Culture Values Lecturette Outline: Does the Difference Make a Difference?", Appendix D, page 239).
2. Provide each participant with a "Differences in Cultural Values" worksheet (Appendix B) and the "Values Differences" handout (Appendix C). Ask each individual to identify on the worksheet where she or he is along the continuum for each value dimension by placing an "X" somewhere on each line.
3. Ask participants to form small groups of 3–5 and discuss the following:
   - Identify a behavior of a co-worker or customer whom you find difficult. Describe the behavior.

   Note: Caution participants not to select a behavior that is a violation of company policy or the law. These are clearly behaviors that cannot be tolerated. Rather, identify one that challenges them personally because of a value they hold. Also caution them to describe the behavior, not interpret what it means. This discussion also assumes the person whose behavior is being described is not present in the training.

- Use the "Differences in Cultural Values" worksheet (Appendix B) to identify a value that the behavior could represent.

Note: Not all values are on this handout, so participants may need to speculate about values that are not listed. Also, behavior is rarely a result of a single value, so they may identify several values for a behavior.

- Which of my personal values may make this particular behavior difficult for me?

Note: Participants should check their own values sheet to see where they placed themselves on a value continuum that they think a behavior might represent. For example, if a member of the group believes someone regularly misses deadlines because he or she values relationships more than task, and one or more group members value task strongly, the differences along this value continuum could make this behavioral difference quite challenging, because it represents a core value difference.

- Does this value/behavior make a difference? For example, does it negatively affect cost, productivity, safety, or legality?
- If so, how might I ask that the behavior be modified?
- If not, how might I modify my response?

4. In the large group, ask each group to share one behavior they identified that did not make a difference and then share how the members of that group thought they could modify their response to it. Also ask them to identify one behavior that did make a difference and share how they decided to ask the other person to modify that behavior.

Debriefing Questions

1. How easy was it to get outside your own behavioral preferences and honestly examine the question "Is this a value-oriented behavior that makes a difference?"
2. When your own value is being challenged by someone else's behavior, how easy is it to examine that value objectively and to consider another perspective?
3. What values were most difficult for you to examine objectively? Why?
4. What have you learned?
5. How can you apply what you learned to the workplace?

Debriefing Conclusions

1. Behavior with which we have difficulty often results from differing values.
2. It is easier to identify troubling behaviors than it is to honestly examine whether such behaviors really make a difference in the workplace.
3. It is not easy to describe someone else's behavior objectively. It is much easier to interpret it from our own values perspective.

4. Many behaviors with which we have difficulty, when examined, are not differences that matter if we can objectively look at them in the workplace context.

5. It is easier to ask others to modify behaviors if they make a difference, especially if we can place the request in the context of workplace productivity, safety, cost, and/or legality.

6. If we can modify our own response when a behavior is not one that matters in the workplace, that adaptation demonstrates a value for diversity.

45

Values Line

Time Required

45–60 minutes (15–30 minutes for activity; 30 minutes for discussion and debriefing)

Objectives

1. To provide participants an opportunity to identify their own values and to explore value differences
2. To explore the difference in meaning and perception that individuals associate with a particular value
3. To experience both similarities and differences in values among people within the same group

Materials

- Values Sets List

Process

1. Introduction: "Each of us has our own perception of what a particular value might mean. If we were to place the values of delegation and control on a continuum, we might be surprised by the discussion that transpires. For some individuals *delegation* means 'I will hand over a project and expect the team or another individual to deliver the result.' For some individuals *delegation* means 'I am going to describe the project, assign specific components to the team or individuals, and then set up periodic checks on progress.' For still other individuals *delegation* means 'I will describe a project and I will actively direct team members and/or individuals until we have finished it.' We all have different comfort levels with delegation and our personal need for control. Our values are often influenced by a variety of factors, such as our degree of accountability for the finished project, our previous experience with delegation, our trust level and past experience with those to whom we are delegating the project, and so on."
2. Ask participants to stand and form a line facing you.
3. Instructions: "We are going to create a human values continuum with one end representing the need for control and the opposite end, a willingness to hand over the project completely. Where would you

fall on the continuum? If you know that you are closer to 'need for control,' move toward your right side; to the left, for more delegation. Begin to discuss your preferences with those nearest to you and determine the order that you should fall into along the continuum, based on your preference."

Address one set of values at a time, using the "Values Sets" list on page 183.

4. Ask participants from each sector of the continuum (left, right, and center) to share their preference and how they determined their placement along the values line. Discussion about previous perceptions of self and others can enrich the activity.

5. Repeat this process for each values set. Use as many as you believe are appropriate.

Debriefing Questions

1. Did you find yourself on the continuum with the same group for most of the values sets?
2. How did you feel about making your choices known to others?
3. Did you have strong feelings about some of the values sets? Why?
4. On the more difficult choices, did you choose honestly or did you feel pressure to alter some of your choices? If so, why?
5. What values made this activity more or less challenging for you?
6. What did you learn?
7. How can you apply what you learned to everyday life?

Debriefing Conclusions

1. Individual similarities and differences in values are likely to exist within any group.
2. We share some values with most other individuals. These shared values tend to be invisible to us unless we find a way to explore them.
3. Unless someone tells us his or her values, we cannot really know them.
4. Our perceptions of someone operating from a different value system are often negative. We need more information to help us understand his or her point of view.

Values Sets List

Money	Power
Time	Money
Security	Risk
Conformity	Nonconformity
Professional Success	Family
Individualism	Group Orientation
Respect for Others	Self-Respect
Tradition	Change
Maintaining Harmony	Resolving Issues
Leadership	Follow the Group
Control	Delegation
Competition	Cooperation
Success	Friendship
Meaningful Work	Recreation
Meeting Deadlines	Doing It Right the First Time

46

The Culture Compass

Adaptable

M–H

P, O, D, M

Time Required

90 minutes (20 minutes to take/score questionnaires; 15 minutes for reading or lecturette; 20 minutes for small groups; 35 minutes for large-group discussion and debriefing)

Objectives

1. To promote understanding of four dimensions of worldviews
2. To identify personal perspectives on each of the four worldviews
3. To identify organizational perspectives on each of the four worldviews
4. To examine how differences in personal perspectives on each of the four worldviews might affect perceptions of others in the workplace
5. To examine how differences in personal and organizational perspectives on the four worldviews might create comfort or discomfort within the organization

Materials

- Personal Perspective Questionnaire and Scoring Sheet; Individual Culture Compass Handout
- Organizational Perspective Questionnaire and Scoring Sheet; Organizational Culture Compass Handout
- Profile of Cultural Perspectives Handout

Process

1. Ask participants to complete, score, and chart their responses to both the "Personal Perspective Questionnaire" and the "Organizational Perspective Questionnaire" on their "Individual Culture Compass" and their "Organizational Culture Compass" handouts.

   Note: Point out to participants that the "most like me" for each item receives a "3" and the "least like me" receives a "1." Also note that items on the scoring sheets are not in numerical order. Otherwise, some participants may move quickly and miss this point in the directions;this can create confusion later.

2. Distribute the "Profile of Cultural Perspectives" handout to each participant. Either allow participants 15 minutes to read this or review the information in a lecturette.

3. Place participants in groups of 3–5 and ask them to compare their personal and organizational culture compasses, looking for both similarities and differences. Ask them to discuss the following questions:
   - How could similarities or differences in your "Personal Culture Compass" affect perceptions of each other and create comfort or discomfort in working or interacting together?
   - What might account for any differences in your "Organizational Culture Compass"?

4. In the large group, discuss observations and implications for potential conflict in the workplace. Ask for suggestions (tools/behaviors) that could result in greater effectiveness.

Debriefing Questions

1. What issues were easier or more difficult for your small group to agree on? Why?

2. How did you feel about completing the compasses? What issues were you most and/or least comfortable discussing? Why?

3. What values—either personal or organizational—affected your responses to this activity? Do areas where your perspective and the organizational perspective differ help you to understand areas where you may be either more or less comfortable working in this organization?

4. What have you learned?

5. How can you use what you have learned in your everyday work life?

Debriefing Conclusions

1. The greater the consistency between personal and organizational values, the greater the satisfaction individuals feel; the less consistency, the greater the potential dissatisfaction.

2. Conflicts or misperceptions between co-workers are often a result of different cultural perspectives.

3. People often perceive the organization's culture differently, based on their roles or responsibilities within the organization.

4. When we can understand the reasons for different cultural perspectives, we can more easily recognize and use the range of perspectives as a resource rather than a source of conflict.

Adapted from an activity by Paula Chu in *Experiential Activities for Intercultural Learning,* edited by H. Ned Seelye.

Personal Perspective Questionnaire

Please rank the following according to similarity with your own perspective.

3—most like me

2—like me

1—least like me

1._____ a. My decisions are primarily guided by what I have learned.

_____ b. I "go with the flow" and adapt my decisions to changing circumstances.

_____ c. When I make a decision, I focus on the result I am looking for.

2._____ a. I tend to take each day as it comes.

_____ b. I tend to keep lists of tasks that I need to accomplish each day.

_____ c. In time things tend to work themselves out.

3._____ a. It is hard for me to stop worrying about upcoming events or deadlines.

_____ b. Life has its own wisdom. Worrying is a waste of my energy.

_____ c. It's best to focus on what today brings and take care of the rest one day at a time.

4._____ a. We are meant to attend to the needs of nature as much as to our own.

_____ b. Our progress and survival depend on our control of natural resources.

_____ c. The power of nature will determine our progress and survival; our power can neither match nature nor truly control it.

5._____ a. In truth we are much better off now that we can make more effective use of our natural resources.

_____ b. For all of our great plans and projects, nature could put mankind in its place in an instant.

_____ c. "Effective use of resources" is the same as "exploitation of the natural world."

6._____ a. No matter where we live, in the country or city, a variety of forces control our destiny.

_____ b. In my life I strive to simplify, which is closer to the natural world.

_____ c. Modern conveniences actually help us appreciate the natural world.

7._____ a. Developing my potential and my sense of self is the most important thing I can do with my life.

_____ b. Being alive and healthy is the most important thing to me; my accomplishments are secondary.

_____ c. It would be a waste if I did not achieve something important in my life.

8._____ a. I prefer to relax and enjoy life as it comes.

_____ b. Peace of mind is possible regardless of external circumstances.

_____ c. I feel useless if I am not doing something constructive with my time.

9._____ a. Taking action is more important than commitment to a belief.

_____ b. We exist only in relation to other people.

_____ c. Being a good person is essential; being successful is not the point.

10._____ a. I've got to be guided by what I think is right, even if I can't please everyone.

_____ b. Having a good leader make the decisions works best; everyone should cooperate accordingly.

_____ c. Decisions affecting a group are more effective if everyone participates in the process.

11._____ a. I respect the individual, not his or her position.

_____ b. Leaders deserve respect because of their position.

_____ c. First and foremost comes unity; people who think of themselves first live at the expense of others.

12._____ a. The head of a group has to take responsibility for its success or failure.

_____ b. If someone in my group is having a problem, I am partly responsible for helping to resolve it.

_____ c. I am accountable for my own successes or failures.

Adapted from an activity by Paula Chu in *Experiential Activities for Intercultural Learning,* edited by H. Ned Seelye.

Personal Perspective Scoring Sheet

Place the number recorded beside each statement in the appropriate space below. Add each row and record the total at the right. Please note that the "order" of the letters changes for each number.

1a _____   +2c _____   +3b _____   =   _____ Past

1b _____   +2a _____   +3c _____   =   _____ Present

1c _____   +2b _____   +3a _____   =   _____ Future

4c _____   +5b _____   +6a _____   =   _____ Yielding

4a _____   +5c _____   +6b _____   =   _____ Harmonious

4b _____   +5a _____   +6c _____   =   _____ Controlling

7c _____   +8c _____   +9a _____   =   _____ Doing

7b _____   +8a _____   +9c _____   =   _____ Being

7a _____   +8b _____   +9b _____   =   _____ Becoming

10a _____   +11a _____   +12c _____   =   _____ Individual

10c _____   +11c _____   +12b _____   =   _____ Mutual

10b _____   +11b _____   +12a _____   =   _____ Ranked

Next you will mark the number corresponding to your score for each subdimension on the Individual Culture Compass. The highest number for each dimension indicates your preferred approach. Shading in each section may enhance score clarity and readability.

Adapted from an activity by Paula Chu in *Experiential Activities for Intercultural Learning,* edited by H. Ned Seelye.

Individual Culture Compass Handout

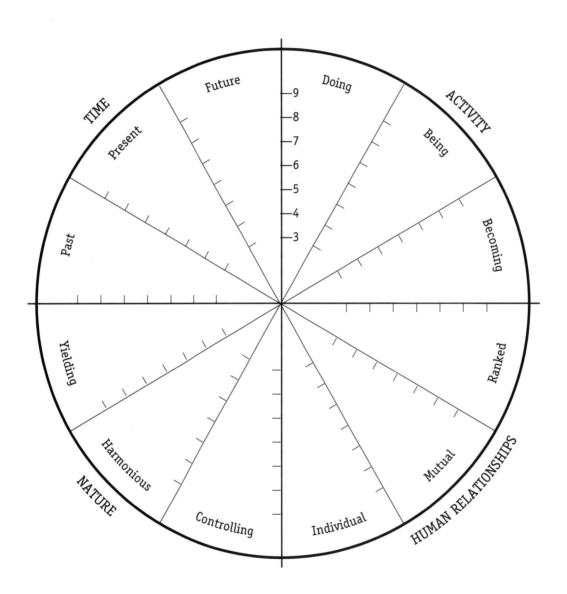

Adapted from an activity by Paula Chu in *Experiential Activities for Intercultural Learning,* edited by H. Ned Seelye.

Organizational Perspective Questionnaire

Please rank the following according to their dominance in your organization.

   3—most dominant

   2—dominant

   1—least dominant

1._____ a. Priorities and strategies are based on tradition and what experience has proven to work.

   _____ b. People tend to "go with the flow."

   _____ c. Priorities and strategies are based on careful consideration of future goals.

2._____ a. The organization as a whole does not emphasize future goals; how it is doing now is more important.

   _____ b. The organization has clear short- and long-term goals that guide daily work.

   _____ c. There is a strong sense of legacy and history in this organization.

3._____ a. In general there is considerable anxiety about upcoming events and deadlines.

   _____ b. There is a great deal of pride in the organization's past accomplishments and reputation.

   _____ c. People in this organization are satisfied with its current state and tend not to worry too much about the future.

4._____ a. The primary purpose of the organization is to contribute to society.

   _____ b. The progress and survival of the organization depend on taking advantage of economic, political, and other opportunities and resources.

   _____ c. The organization is relatively powerless in the large scheme of things.

5._____ a. Effective management and use of resources enable the organization to influence and control its destiny.

   _____ b. The organization has little control, given the many constraints under which it must operate.

   _____ c. The organization has a mutually beneficial relationship with its political, economic, and social environments.

6._____ a. The organization is seen as a small cog in a very complex machine.

   _____ b. The organization exists to cooperate with and further the goals of its larger cultural environment.

_____ c. In the organization it is believed that goals can be achieved through hard work, perseverance, and seizing opportunities as they arise.

7. _____ a. The organization emphasizes employee development.

_____ b. The organization is able to employ people who like to work here and don't see the need for employee development.

_____ c. The organization emphasizes getting the job done as the top priority.

8. _____ a. If difficulty or problems are encountered, it is assumed that things will work themselves out.

_____ b. Problems that arise here are seen as a natural part of the growth and development of any organization; everyone has his or her role in solving them.

_____ c. If a difficulty arises, it must be resolved immediately; ignoring it is seen as counterproductive.

9. _____ a. What the organization stands for is considered less important than getting one's work done well.

_____ b. People work here because the work accomplished is important.

_____ c. All employees are encouraged to be themselves; that is their best contribution to the organization.

10. _____ a. Each person makes decisions based on what seems right.

_____ b. Those in positions of authority make the decisions; everyone else follows those directives.

_____ c. Decision making is, for the most part, a collective process.

11. _____ a. Everyone here is considered worthy of equal respect.

_____ b. Those at the top of the hierarchy are worthy of respect because of their positions.

_____ c. People who try to gain for themselves alone do so at the expense of others.

12. _____ a. The head of the department guides the rest of the unit and takes responsibility for its successes and failures.

_____ b. If someone has a success or a failure, the responsibility is shared by others in the department.

_____ c. Each person is held accountable for his or her own successes and failures.

Adapted from an activity by Paula Chu in _Experiential Activities for Intercultural Learning,_ edited by H. Ned Seelye.

Organizational Perspective Scoring Sheet

Place the number recorded beside each statement in the appropriate space below and add to the right.

1a ____	+2c ____	+3b ____	=	____ Past
1b ____	+2a ____	+3c ____	=	____ Present
1c ____	+2b ____	+3a ____	=	____ Future
4c ____	+5b ____	+6a ____	=	____ Yielding
4a ____	+5c ____	+6b ____	=	____ Harmonious
4b ____	+5a ____	+6c ____	=	____ Controlling
7c ____	+8c ____	+9a ____	=	____ Doing
7b ____	+8a ____	+9c ____	=	____ Being
7a ____	+8b ____	+9b ____	=	____ Becoming
10a ____	+11a ____	+12c ____	=	____ Individual
10c ____	+11c ____	+12b ____	=	____ Mutual
10b ____	+11b ____	+12a ____	=	____ Ranked

Next you will mark the number corresponding to your score for each subdimension on the Organizational Culture Compass. The highest number for each dimension indicates the organization's preferred approach. Shading in each section may enhance score clarity and readability.

Adapted from an activity by Paula Chu in *Experiential Activities for Intercultural Learning*, edited by H. Ned Seelye.

Organizational Culture Compass Handout

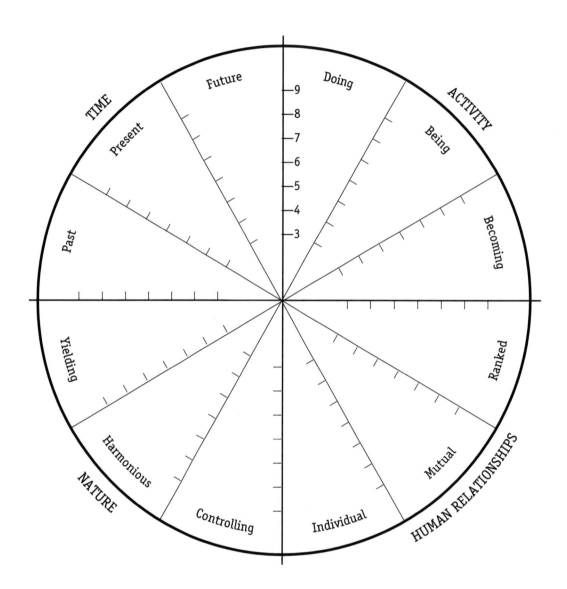

Adapted from an activity by Paula Chu in *Experiential Activities for Intercultural Learning,* edited by H. Ned Seelye.

Profile of Cultural Perspectives Handout

Compare your individual and organizational compasses with the following profile of cultural perspectives.

A. Orientation toward Time

- Past
- Present
- Future

Past

Assumption:	Today flows out of the legacy of the past.
Finds meaning in:	Serenity, surrender, history as context and teacher
Meaning of work:	Work is a place to establish and nurture relationships and traditions. There is an awareness of, connection to, and obligation toward the legacy of such relationships and traditions.

Present

Assumption:	Today is the only reality.
Finds meaning in:	*Carpe diem* ("Seize the day").
Meaning of work:	Work, like life, is to be enjoyed. Present-oriented individuals often bring to work an energy and vitality not frequently embodied by the other orientations.

Future

Assumption:	Today is a step toward tomorrow's goals.
Finds meaning in:	Establishing and working toward goals, work ethic
Meaning of work:	The individual finds his or her identity through achievements in the workplace. One keeps one's eye on deadlines and goals and evaluates the present in relation to its utility in moving toward the future. One is rarely satisfied with achievements, focusing on the next goal instead. The ethic "no pain, no gain" is endorsed.

B. Orientation toward the Environment/Nature

- Yielding
- Harmonious
- Controlling

Yielding

Assumption:	Nature is in charge of life on earth.
Finds meaning in:	Turning control over to nature
Meaning of work:	Work must be done. Within an organization individuals may feel dominated by the organization and try to adapt to their roles and assignments rather than influence them.

Harmonious

Assumption:	Our relationship with nature is symbiotic; care of the physical world will pay off with a balanced and peaceful existence.
Finds meaning in:	Harmony, doing one's share
Meaning of work:	Work is part of a natural balance wherein people contribute to a symbiotic relationship between society and nature as part of their responsibility for being given life.

Controlling

Assumption:	Human welfare is primary; nature serves to meet individuals' needs.
Finds meaning in:	Taking charge of challenges, mind over matter, effective use of resources
Meaning of work:	Work is a place to manage and control tasks, resources, and employees. Problems are to be solved, knots in the system untied, hurdles jumped or dismantled.

C. Orientation Toward Activity

- Doing
- Being
- Becoming

Doing

Assumption:	Taking action is the most important activity.
Finds meaning in:	Accomplishments, achievements
Meaning of work:	A person is what she or he *does*. Work is pursued for a living.
	Relationships are secondary to the task. Work and play are separate activities, but "doers" often work hard and play hard (Work = Living).

Being

Assumption:	Self-expression is the most important activity.
Finds meaning in:	Spontaneous expression, being oneself, affiliation
Meaning of work:	Work is not directly attached to the ego, nor is it strictly considered a separate activity from leisure. Social and work relationships may be closely intertwined.
	Relationship development at work is time well spent. It builds morale and group identity.

Becoming

Assumption:	Self-development is the most important activity.
Finds meaning in:	Process, purpose, and intention of activity
Meaning of work:	A person is deeply invested in the *type of work* and its process; both aspects add to one's personal development.

D. Orientation toward Human Relationships

- Individual
- Mutual
- Ranked

Individual

Assumption:	Each person is responsible for what happens in his or her life and must watch out for his or her own rights and welfare.
Finds meaning in:	Personal accountability, competitive ethic
Meaning of work:	Work is a place to be recognized for one's achievements. Upward mobility and other forms of recognition are expected by employees. Group goals, rewards, and achievements are not as satisfying.

Mutual

Assumption:	Each person's purpose is to make a contribution to a larger world.
Finds meaning in:	Interdependence, group goals, affiliation
Meaning of work:	Work is a place to make a contribution to a group effort. The individual needs to have a sense of being a part of projects and to see the connection to a larger goal or effort. Public praise and competition among or comparison with others may cause embarrassment.

Ranked

Assumption:	Each of us has his or her own place, and respect is due according to one's position.
Finds meaning in:	Tradition, hierarchy, family, protocol
Meaning of work:	Work is a place to enhance or strengthen but not necessarily to advance one's social position. Protocol is seen as maintaining the social fabric.
	There is a higher value placed on being respectful than on being frank.

Adapted from an activity by Paula Chu in *Experiential Activities for Intercultural Learning*, edited by H. Ned Seelye.

47

Values of Conflict

General

M–H

P, T, D, M

Time Required

90 minutes (5 minutes for rank ordering; 30 minutes for group consensus; 20 minutes for reporting to large group and group discussion; 35 minutes for debriefing)

Objectives

1. To experience how different people evaluate the same situation
2. To participate in group decision making regarding a conflict
3. To identify the values that influence how we evaluate conflict

Materials

- Perception and Conflict Handout
- Two flipcharts
- Marking pens

Process

1. Write the names (or job title, in one case) of the six people in the "Perception and Conflict" handout down the left side of an easel page. Then write group numbers across the sheet for as many groups as will be doing this activity.

Name	Group 1	Group 2	Group 3	Group 4
Mr. Nguyen				
Recreation Manager				
Charles				
Tom				
Peter				
Mai				

2. Provide each participant with a copy of the "Perception and Conflict" handout. Give them approximately five minutes to individually read and then rank order the six people in the story from best to worst. The person who "acted the best or most honorably" receives a "1," and the one who "acted the worst or least honorably" gets a "6." No "ties" are allowed.

   Note: This story can be rewritten to fit the environment of the group you will be working with. We have written it for public libraries, manufacturing plants, public schools, and so forth.

The important elements to include in your story are: six people: one person who has responsibility for the "rules" (the recreation manager, in this story), the leaders of two opposing groups (Mr. Nguyen and Charles), someone who uses a harsh racial insult (Tom), someone who hears the insult and says nothing (Peter), and someone who damages someone's property (Mai).

3. Place participants in groups of 4–6 and give the groups 30 minutes to share their rankings and come to a consensus ranking based on their discussions.
4. Returning to the larger group, ask each small group to report their rankings and record them on the chart you have made on the easel.
5. Identify any name that received identical rankings across groups. For example, Mr. Nguyen is very often ranked highest by everyone. Ask the participants to identify why he was ranked so highly. While participants are discussing their reasons for ranking this person(s) the way they did, listen carefully for values and write them on another easel sheet. For example, you may hear Mr. Nguyen's top ranking as justified because of his responsibility, leadership, and rule-governed behavior. Do the same for other identical rankings.
6. Now identify any names that received different rankings across the groups and ask the groups to explain their decisions. Again, as you listen to the justifications, write any values you hear on the second flipchart. For example, Mai is often ranked "2" because she didn't tolerate racism, or "6" because she retaliated in kind by destroying property. On the easel you could write social justice or retaliation. Follow this process with each of the six names in the story.
7. Ask the participants what they notice about the similarities and differences of values identified on the second flipchart. For example, one group may have ranked Peter as "1" or "2" because he did nothing but observe, while another group might have ranked him as "6" because he failed to act on his own values. The recreation manager may have been ranked "1" or "2" by one group because he only enforced the rules, but other groups may have ranked him "6" because he was responsible for the facility, he did not take charge of the situation, and he even gave conflicting messages.

Debriefing Questions

1. How did you feel as you read this story? What issues emerged for you?
2. What happened during the small-group discussions? Did anyone take over leadership of the group?
3. Was your group able to come to an agreement on the rankings? If not, what happened?
4. What were the areas of most/least difficulty in coming to consensus about the rankings? Why?
5. Which of your personal values were most challenged as you read the story, participated in the small group discussions, and listened to other groups' rankings?

6. What have you learned?
7. How can you apply what you learned to your everyday life?

Debriefing Conclusions

1. Our personal values influence how we evaluate situations and people.
2. It is difficult to reach consensus when we hold different values.
3. If we listen carefully to another person's point of view—and the reasons for it—we can often find common values and come to agreement.
4. We are often inclined to get into polarized discussions about "right" or "wrong" rather than listening to understand others' views.
5. It is most difficult to attain consensus when one or more people hold very strong values about an issue (e.g., social justice, responsibility, lack of respect for public property, etc.)

Perception and Conflict Handout

A family of Vietnamese has come to a forest camp. Mr. Nguyen goes to the recreation manager to ask if they may use the recreation facility on Monday evening for traditional dancing. The manager says yes. Monday evening arrives and the Vietnamese enter the recreation facility to find a large group of young men already using the facility. When Mr. Nguyen approaches Charles, the apparent leader of the group, a confrontation ensues. Charles says the recreation facility is "first come, first served" and they were there first. The Vietnamese leave.

The next morning Mr. Nguyen approaches the recreation manager and explains the problem. The manager states that there had been a mistake, that the recreation facility is, in fact, first come, first served. Mr. Nguyen is told he will need to find another place for his activities. That evening when the same group of young men enter the facility, they find that the Vietnamese are already there and have begun their dancing. Another confrontation occurs between Charles and Mr. Nguyen, during which Tom, one of the young men, shouts, "Why don't you damned gooks just go back where you belong." Peter, one of the young men, feels very bad about the confrontation and the comment but says nothing.

The young men leave the facility but go to the Vietnamese' campsite and dump garbage all over it. When Mai, one of the Vietnamese, hears what has happened, she gets angry and smashes the headlight on one of the young men's cars.

The recreation manager is called in to resolve the situation.

48

Working with Values

Time Required

80 minutes (5 minutes for brief overview; 15 minutes for personal ranking; 30 minutes for small-group discussion; 30 minutes for large-group discussion and debriefing)

Objectives

1. To identify and rank order 18 personal values
2. To identify the values of the organization, the department, or the work team
3. To compare the alignment of personal values with the identified values of the organization, department, or work team
4. To discuss the potential impact of the degree of alignment of personal and organizational, departmental, or team values
5. To discuss the cause and effect of individuals having different perceptions of the organization's values

Materials

- A flipchart and marking pens or an overhead projector and transparency
- A Rokeach Values Rankings Worksheet for each participant

Process

1. Give a brief overview of terminal and instrumental values (see Appendix A, "Culture and Values Narrative," page 231) and a clarification of the usefulness of an understanding of values.
   a. Two Types of Values
      - *Terminal values* represent the goal we want to achieve.
      - *Instrumental values* are the behaviors we use to get to the goal.
      - Individuals can have *similar terminal values and act differently.* For example, family may be a value for two people—one person demonstrates that value via his nuclear family; the other demonstrates it through her extended family.
      - Individuals can have *different terminal values but act the same.* For example, two people work hard to make a lot of money. One individual saves her money to support her value of security,

while the other person spends his money to support his value of demonstrating material success.

  b. The Usefulness of Understanding Values
    • Values help us to understand and interpret events.
    • Values provide a framework for making decisions.
    • Values provide a framework for carrying out decisions.

2. Give each participant a copy of the "Rokeach Values Rankings" worksheet. In the first column, ask participants to rank order their personal values from 1–18 based on the boldface "Terminal Values" category. Allow time for everyone to complete the task. Now direct participants to rank order the values for the organization in the second column. Again, focus on the boldface "Terminal Values," categories. Finally, have participants review the description of behaviors, or instrumental values, under each terminal value and make any changes they would like. For example, they might add "work hard to help the team succeed at its defined goals" under "ambitious."

3. Place participants in groups of 3–5. Write the following questions on a flipchart or a transparency and ask the groups to discuss them.
    • If there are any areas where personal and organizational values are not aligned, what impact might this have on the individual? On the effectiveness of the organization?
    • Are there any terminal values about which you and the larger organization could have different behavioral expectations?
    • If any of you have different rankings for the organizational values, discuss those rankings and identify why you might have different perceptions.
    • How will the perceptions of the organization's values affect planning processes? Personnel policies? Decision making? Conflict management?

      Note: You can add specific areas based on any issues you know are currently prominent in the organization or the team with which you are working.

4. Return to the large group; ask each small group to report the results of its discussion. Debrief.

Debriefing Questions

1. How closely aligned are your own values with those of the organization?
2. In the small-group discussions, did you find that the perceptions of organizational values were consistent or inconsistent across members of the group? What was the reasoning behind the choices?
3. How did you feel about sharing your personal value choices? Why?
4. What values affected your participation in this activity? Why?
5. What values did you see demonstrated by group members as they participated?
6. What have you learned?
7. How could you apply information from this experience to your work

life?

8. What actions could follow that would make this information most useful to the organization?

Debriefing Conclusions

1. An individual is likely to experience greater job satisfaction when there is congruency between individual and organizational values.
2. Individuals may have different perceptions of an organization's values depending on their job, their organizational placement, or their supervisor.
3. Understanding the organization's values can help employees interpret events within the organization.
4. Understanding personal and organizational values can contribute to effective organizational performance, including decision making, planning, personnel actions, and conflict-management processes.
5. Actions that are seen as congruent with organizational values are most likely to be rewarded.
6. If team members have congruent perceptions of their values, the team is most likely to perform well.

Optional Process

For team building with an intact work team (additional materials required are easel pages listing the 18 instrumental values [allowing room for sticky dots] and large red and yellow sticky dots in sets of ten).

1. Prepare a wall chart of the 18 values with room on the side for the placement of sticky dots.
2. As in the main process, supply participants with a copy of the worksheet and ask them to rank order their personal values and those of the organization.
3. Prior to small-group discussions, provide each participant with 20 large sticky dots (10 red and 10 yellow). Ask participants to place the red dots next to their top 10 personal values and the yellow dots next to what they believe to be the organization's or team's top 10 values.
4. Based on the visual created, ask the small groups to identify and discuss where the team's potential areas of strength, challenge, or conflict might surface. Ask them to identify specific strategies or behaviors they can use to reduce areas of potential conflict.

Rokeach Values Rankings Worksheet

Personal Rank 1–18 1=high	Organizational Rank 1–18; 1=high	TERMINAL VALUES: Goals Instrumental Values: Behaviors
		AMBITIOUS Work hard to get ahead/succeed
		BROAD-MINDED Listen to a wide range of perspectives; change my mind based on others' ideas
		CAPABLE Skilled and effective at a job or task(s)
		CLEAN Neat/tidy
		COURAGEOUS Stand up for my beliefs—even when unpopular
		FORGIVING Willing to pardon others
		HELPFUL Work for the welfare of others
		HONEST Tell the truth even if it is unpopular or difficult
		IMAGINATIVE Creative—can see "outside the box"
		INDEPENDENT Self-reliant/self-sufficient; work well alone
		INTELLECTUAL Able to understand both the "what" and the "why"
		LOGICAL Consistent/rational in approaching issues
		LOVING Affectionate/tender; think about others
		LOYAL Faithful to friends or the group
		OBEDIENT Follow the rules
		POLITE Use "please" and "thank you"
		RESPONSIBLE Always follow through on commitments
		SELF-CONTROLLED Restrained and self-disciplined

Adapted from Dr. Van Hutton's presentation on the work of Milton Rokeach, Seattle University, Seattle Washington, 1998.

49

Top Two

Time Required
60 minutes (15 minutes for individual work; 20 minutes for small-group discussion; 25 minutes for debriefing)

Objectives
1. To identify priority values for individuals
2. To identify behaviors that reflect those core values
3. To discuss commonalities and differences among group members and how these can affect work relationships

Materials
- Top Values List for each participant
- Two index cards for each participant

Process
1. Provide participants with a copy of the "Top Values" list and ask them to select 20 that are most important to them individually.
2. Next instruct participants to reduce the list to the 10 most important values from their list.
3. Then ask them to select the 5 most important values from their list. *(Note: Be prepared for groans and protests.)*
4. Now ask participants to select the 2 most important values from their list of 5 and write each value on a separate index card. On the back of each card instruct them to write two behaviors they exhibit (at work) that support that value.
5. Place participants in groups of 3–4. Each individual will share the 2 values written on his or her index card, discuss reasons for giving this value such a high priority, and ask others to describe behaviors that they would expect to see (at work) from someone holding that value. If any behaviors shared by the group are inconsistent with what the individual has written on the card, they will discuss those differences for the purpose of understanding each other.
6. Bring participants back together for debriefing.

Debriefing Questions

1. How did you feel as you were selecting your top 20 values? As you were asked to reduce the list—first to 10, then to 5, and finally to 2?
2. How did you feel as you listened to others' values? As you listened to others describe behavior associated with your values?
3. Describe the similarities and differences in your small group. What did you notice about the group dynamics as you identified similarities versus differences?
4. What values do you hold that made this activity easy or difficult?
5. What have you learned?
6. How could you apply information from this experience to your work life?

Debriefing Conclusions

1. Prioritizing values is difficult because all of our values are important to us.
2. Individuals from the same cultural background and same organization may hold very different values.
3. Individuals who hold the same value may act out that value differently.
4. Discussion of similarities and differences in values can enrich the working relationship by fostering better understanding and an atmosphere of respect and acceptance. This is particularly true if the objective of the discussion is to *understand* the differences, not to judge them.

Optional Debriefing Questions

If the group is an intact work team, ask them to discuss the following questions:

1. What similarities or differences do we have in either values or behaviors that can benefit our team? How and why?
2. What are the similarities or differences in either values or behaviors that could be a disadvantage to our team? How and why?
3. What specific actions can we take to maximize the advantages and minimize or eliminate the disadvantages?

Adapted from an activity in *The Whole World Guide to Culture Learning* by J. Daniel Hess.

Top Values List

Simplicity	Tradition	Technology
Unity	Collaboration	Authenticity
Security	Competence	Ritual
Community	Adaptability	Solitude
Reflection	Innovation	Dexterity
Duty	Patience	Profit
Efficiency	Empathy	Diversity
Generosity	Stewardship	Wisdom
Accountability	Curiosity	Family
Global Harmony	Expansion	Education
Order	Confidence	Creativity
Control	Playfulness	Justice
Expressiveness	Discernment	Flexibility
Knowledge	Independence	Acceptance
Intimacy	Celebration	Equality
Congruency	Obedience	Patriotism
Loyalty	Beauty	Compassion
Discipline	Honor	Achievement
Social Responsibility	Self-Actualization	Social Affirmation
Belonging	Health	Respect
Honesty	Innovation	Integration
Ownership	Communication	Prestige
Recreation	Human Dignity	Productivity
Interdependence	Vision	Service
Quality	Success	Workmanship

Adapted from an activity in *The Whole World Guide to Culture Learning* by J. Daniel Hess.

50

Survey Your Values

Time Required
90 minutes (25 minutes for completion and scoring of survey; 15 minutes for lecturette; 20 minutes for small-group discussion; 20 minutes for large-group discussion; 10 minutes for debriefing)

Objectives
1. To examine personal values in four separate orientations: activity, time, human relations, and nature
2. To identity how differences in these orientations across a workforce or team can affect workplace behaviors, perceptions, and relationships
3. To identify how differences in these orientations can affect families and cooperation in a work or campus setting

Materials
- Value Orientations Survey
- Value Orientations Survey Scoring Sheet

Process
1. Ask participants to complete and score the "Value Orientations Survey." *(Note: It is important for participants to identify a "common other" before they begin to take the survey, e.g., work team, global organization, generational family, and so forth.)*
2. Provide a lecturette on the four separate value orientations (refer to Appendix C, "Values Differences" handout on page 235 for information from which to draw lecturette material).
3. Place participants in small groups of 4–6 people and ask them to compare their responses, looking for areas of similarity and difference. Specifically discuss how both similarities and differences are likely to affect their workplace behaviors, perceptions of each other, and relationships.
4. While they are still in their small groups, ask participants to also discuss areas where each individual in the group believes he or she is different from most others in the organization. *(Note: You may find differences based on articulated values versus observable behaviors.)* Tell the groups to look for any implications this may have for how

that person might modify behavior in the workplace and/or areas where she or he might feel either more or less comfortable in the organization.

5. Return to the larger group and discuss areas of similarities identified in the small groups. What advantages or disadvantages might this offer the team or the organization? Where did they find differences? What advantages or disadvantages does this offer the team or the organization?

Debriefing Questions

1. Describe your experience in taking the "Value Orientations Survey." Which questions were easier to answer? Harder? Why?
2. How do you feel about the values at the opposite ends of the continua from yourself? How might this relate to your experience of people who are culturally different as either co-workers or customers?
3. What values did you identify that might challenge you while working in this organization? With specific co-workers? Specific types of customers?
4. What have you learned?
5. How can you apply information from this experience to your work life?

Debriefing Conclusions

1. Cultural values are often unconscious and frame our view of reality.
2. Value orientations can be described in terms of activity, time, relationships, and nature. These orientations can be described on a continuum.
3. When we encounter someone with different values or behaviors we are often confused, uncomfortable, or irritated.
4. Becoming aware of our own values and cultural perspectives can increase our understanding of the behavior of those who hold different values.

Adapted from the Kluckhohn "Value Orientations Survey" in *Finding the Middle Ground: Insights and Applications of the Value Orientations Method*, edited by Kurt W. Russo.

Value Orientations Survey

From each of the following general life situations please pick the best personal solution or choice for you. Also select the response that you believe most others in your organization (team, family, program) would choose as "best." Record your choices on the "Value Orientations Survey Answer Sheet."

1. Job Choice

You are in need of employment and have the opportunity to work for two different bosses. These two bosses are very different. Which would be the best one to work for?

A. One boss is fair with employees and offers a higher wage than others, but this boss expects employees to work hard and stick to the job. This boss does not like an employee to take unscheduled time off for a trip or to have a day of fun. Should that happen, this boss does not believe it is right to keep that employee on the job.

B. This boss pays an average wage but is not so strict. This boss understands that employees may need unscheduled time off to take a trip or to have a day of fun. Even when an employee does not show up for work, this boss keeps the employee without saying too much.

Which boss would you prefer?	A	B
Which boss do you believe others in your organization (team, family, program) would prefer?	A	B

2. Child Training

A group of individuals are discussing the way that children should be brought up. Here are three different ideas:

A. It is important for children to be taught the traditions of the past. We learn from the past, and the old ways have value. When children do not know or understand about the traditions of the past, they have no guide to follow and they get into trouble.

B. Children should be taught some of the old traditions, but it is wrong to insist that they stick to these ways. It is equally important for children to learn about new ways and to take on the ways that will best help them get along in today's world.

C. It is not so important that children be taught much about past traditions except as an interesting story of what has gone before. It is best for children to learn new ways of doing things.

Which of these ideas do you most agree with?	A	B	C
Which of these ideas do you believe most people in your organization (team, family, program) would agree with?	A	B	C

3. Livestock Dying

A landowner had a small herd of cattle. Over a short period of time, most of the animals died in different ways. When this was discussed, people had different things to say about what had happened.

A. Some people said the landowner was not to blame. Sometimes things like this just happen, and it is not possible to prevent such losses. It is important that we all learn to take the bad with the good.

B. Some people said it was the landowner's fault that so many animals were lost. The landowner did not act to prevent the losses. Landowners who keep up with the new ways of doing things can almost always find a way to prevent such losses.

C. Some people said that it was probably because the landowner did not live "right"—had not acted in a way that promoted harmony with the forces of nature.

Which of these reasons do you think is usually true?	A	B	C
Which of these reasons do you believe most people in your organization (team, family, program) would agree with?	A	B	C

4. Housework

Two women were talking about the way they liked to live.
  A. One woman said she liked to find extra things to do that were of interest to her. She said she was happiest when she kept busy and got many things done.
  B. The other woman said she was willing to work, but she didn't like to spend too much time doing extra things. She liked to have free time to visit friends, take trips, and talk with whomever was around.

Which of these two is most like you?	A	B
Which of these two is most like other people in your organization (team, family, program)?	A	B

5. Expectations about Change

Three young people shared their thoughts on what their own families would have one day as compared with their mothers and fathers. They each had different things to say.
  A. The first person said, "I expect my family's circumstances to be about the same as my parents' family circumstances. It is best to work hard and plan ways to keep things as they have been in the past."
  B. The second person said, "I don't know whether my family will be better off, the same, or worse off than my parents' family. Things always go up and down. Even if people work hard, you can never really tell how things will go."
  C. The third person said, "I expect my family will be better off in the future than my parents' family. If I work hard and plan well, I can expect that things will continue to get better in relation to how hard I try."

Which of these people do you most agree with?	A	B	C
Which of these people do you believe most people in your organization (team, family, program) would agree with?	A	B	C

6. Facing Conditions

There are different ways of thinking about God (or the gods) in relation to people, the weather, and all other natural conditions that cause crops or animals to live or die. Here are three possibilities.
  A. We cannot really know how God (or the gods) will use power over all of the natural conditions that affect the crops and animals. It is useless to think we can change conditions very much or for very long. It is best to take conditions as they come and to do the best we can with them.
  B. God (or the gods) does (do) not directly control all of the conditions that affect the growth of crops or animals. It is up to us to figure out the ways to understand the conditions and to try to control them.

C. God (or the gods) and people work together all the time. The good or bad conditions that affect the crops and animals depend on whether we make choices that keep us in harmony with God (or the gods) and with the forces of nature.

Which of these ideas do you most agree with?	A	B	C
Which of these ideas do you believe most people in your organization (team, family, program) would agree with?	A	B	C

7. Help in Misfortune

A family has just had a severe loss in the stock market. They are going to need help from someone to get through the next several months. There are several options for getting the help they need. Here are three possible choices.
  A. It would be best to go to the boss or a close, older relative who is used to managing things and to ask for help until things get better.
  B. It would be best to try to earn some extra money on their own.
  C. It would be best to depend on brothers, sisters, or other relatives to help out as much as possible.

Which way of getting help do you think is best?	A	B	C
Which of the three ways do you think most other people in your organization (team, family, program) would choose?	A	B	C

8. Family Work Relations

Here are three different ways that families who are related and live close together can arrange work.
  A. Families that are closely related work together, and the oldest able person is responsible for and takes charge of most of the important things.
  B. Close relatives in families work together to take care of whatever problems come up. Whenever a problem arises, the most able person is chosen to handle the problem, regardless of age.
  C. Each family member (husband, wife, and children) looks after his or her own business and is not responsible for the other family members.

Which of these ways do you think is usually best?	A	B	C
Which of the three ways do you think most people in your organization (team, family, program) would say is best?	A	B	C

9. Choice of a Delegate

An organization similar to yours is going to send a delegate or representative to a meeting. How should the delegate be chosen?
  A. It is important for the older, influential leaders to take responsibility for deciding who should represent the organization. After all, they have the most experience in such matters.
  B. It is best to call everyone together for a meeting to discuss the situation until almost everyone agrees prior to taking a vote to elect the representative.
  C. It is best to call a meeting, ask for names of likely representatives, then vote for the best candidate. The person winning the majority of the votes will represent everyone, even though there may be many people still opposed to this person.

Which of these ways of choosing a delegate do you like best?	A	B	C
Which of the three ways do you think most people in your organization (team, family, program) would use?	A	B	C

10. Maintenance of Gardens

Three vegetable gardeners have different ways of planting and taking care of crops.
  A. One puts the plants in and works sufficiently hard but does not do more than necessary. This person believes that the results depend mainly on the weather conditions and nothing that people do can change things very much.
  B. One person puts in crops and then works hard to have a good harvest, making use of all of the scientific advances available. This person believes that by using scientific methods, many of the bad conditions can be prevented.
  C. One puts in crops, works hard, and tries to live in a proper way. This person believes that keeping in harmony with the forces of nature has the greatest effect on the condition of the crops.

Which of these ways do you most agree with?	A	B	C
Which of these ways do you think most people in your organization (team, family, program) would agree with?	A	B	C

11. Philosophy of Life

People often have very different ideas about what has gone on before and what we can expect from life. Here are three ways to think about life.
  A. Some people believe that the ways of the past (traditional ways) are the best. Things get worse as they change. These people believe that it is important to keep the old ways alive, and when those ways are lost, they try to bring them back.
  B. Some people believe it is most important to pay attention to the present. They say the past is gone and the future is too uncertain. When things change, it is sometimes for the better and sometimes for the worse. These people see value in some of the old ways but are ready to accept new ways that make life easier and better.
  C. Some people believe that the new and future ways are almost always best in the long run. They believe that the best way to live is to look ahead and give up things in the present so that the future will be better.

Which of these ways of looking at life do you think is best?	A	B	C
Which of these ways of looking at life do you believe most people in your organization (team, family, program) would say is best?	A	B	C

12. Wage Work

People may choose to work in many different ways. Here are three ways they might work.
  A. Some people prefer to work for a boss who owns his own business and has been running things for a long time. People working in this situation may not take part in deciding how the business should be run, but they know that they can depend on the boss to help them in many ways.
  B. Some people like to be part of a group in which everyone has something to say in the decisions that are made and everyone can count on each other.

C. Some people like to work on their own, as individuals. People working in this situation make their own decisions and expect to take care of themselves.

Which of these ways of working sounds most satisfying to you?	A	B	C
Which of these three ways do you think most people in your organization (team, family, program) would say is best?	A	B	C

13. Belief in Control

Three people from different geographical areas were discussing things that affect the weather and control other conditions. Here is what they said.
A. "We have never controlled the weather or other natural conditions, and we probably never will. There have always been good years and bad years. It is wisest to take things as they come and just do the best we can."
B. "We believe it is our job to find ways to overcome weather and other conditions. We believe we can succeed in overcoming droughts and floods just as we have overcome many other things."
C. "We can keep things going by working with the forces that cause weather and other conditions. It is when we live in the proper way—doing what we can to keep the land, water, and so on in good condition—that all goes well."

Which of these people do you most agree with?	A	B	C
Which of these people do you believe most people in your organization (team, family, program) would say had the best idea?	A	B	C

14. Ceremonial Innovation

People in your community have begun to notice that religious traditions are changing.
A. Some people are unhappy with the change. They feel that religious traditions should be kept exactly as they have been in the past.
B. Some people prefer the old religious traditions, but they realize that hanging on to them causes too many problems. It is easier to accept the changes as they happen.
C. Some people are really pleased with the changes to the religious traditions. They believe that the new ways are usually better than the old ways, and they like to keep things moving ahead.

Which of these ideas do you most agree with?	A	B	C
Which of the three ways of thinking do you believe most other people in your organization (team, family, program) would agree with?	A	B	C

15. Ways of Living

Two people were talking about how they liked to live.
A. One person said, "What I care about most is accomplishing things. I like to get things done, to see results."
B. The other person said, "What I care most about is having time to myself. The best way for me to live is to be true to my own nature and enjoy life."

Which of these two people do you most agree with?	A	B
Which of these two people do you think most people in your organization (team, family, program) would most agree with?	A	B

16. Land Inheritance

A woman who recently died left some land to her sons and daughters. All of these sons and daughters are adults, and they all live near each other. Here are three choices for how they might handle the property.
  A. The oldest son or daughter is expected to take charge of the land and to manage it for himself or herself as well as for the others in the family who have a share.
  B. All of the sons and daughters should make use of the land together. When a leader is needed, they choose one (not necessarily the oldest) to take charge.
  C. Each son or daughter should take his or her share of the land and do with it what he or she wants. Alternatively, they may all decide to sell the property and split the profits equally.

Which of these ways do you think is usually best?	A	B	C
Which of these three ways do you think most other people in your organization (team, family, program) would say is best?	A	B	C

17. Care of Fields

There were two farmers who lived differently.
  A. One farmer always put in extra time to keep the fields clear of weeds and in fine condition. Because of this extra work, the farmer did not have much time left for friends, for vacations, or for enjoying life in other ways.
  B. The other farmer kept the crops growing but didn't do any more work than absolutely necessary. This farmer did have time to spend with friends, go on vacations, and enjoy life.

Which person is it better to be?	A	B
Which person do you think most people in your organization (team, family, program) would say it is better to be?	A	B

18. Length of Life

Three people were talking about whether it is possible for doctors and scientists to significantly lengthen the lives of men and women.
  A. One person said, "I really do not believe that there is much that human beings can do to make their lives longer. Every person has a set time to live, and when the time comes to die, it comes."
  B. Another person said, "Doctors and scientists are already finding ways to help people live longer by discovering new medicines, introducing vaccines, and studying diet. If people pay attention to new scientific discoveries, they will likely live longer."
  C. The third person said, "I believe that there is a plan to life that works to keep all things moving together. If people learn to live their lives according to that plan, they will live longer than other men and women."

Which of these ideas do you most agree with?	A	B	C
Which of the three ways of thinking do you believe most people in your organization (team, family, program) would agree with?	A	B	C

19. Water Allocation

The government plans to help a community get more water by redrilling and cleaning out a community well. The government officials suggest that the community develop its own plan for dividing the additional water. Since the amount of extra water is not yet known, people feel differently about planning.

A. Some say that whatever water becomes available should be divided just as it was in the past.
B. Others want to wait until the extra water becomes available before deciding how it will be divided.
C. The rest want to work out a plan ahead of time for dividing whatever extra water becomes available.

Which of these ways do you think is best?	A	B	C
Which of the three ways do you think most others in your organization (team, family, program) would say is best?	A	B	C

20. Nonworking Time

Two men spend their time in different ways when they are not working.

A. One man spends most of his time learning new things or trying things that will help him in his work.
B. The other man spends most of his time talking with friends and visiting new places.

Which of these men is most like you?	A	B
Which of these men do you think is most like other people in your organization (team, family, program)?	A	B

*** END OF SURVEY ***

Adapted from the Kluckhohn "Value Orientations Survey" in *Finding the Middle Ground: Insights and Applications of the Value Orientations Method*, edited by Kurt W. Russo.

Value Orientations Survey Scoring Sheet

Directions: Enter the letter that represents your choices (you/others in your organization, team, family, program) for each situation. At the bottom of each column, total the number of each letter (e.g., A=3, B=2, C=3) in that column. The totals will give you your values tendency for each dimension. You will then be able to compare similarities and differences with "others" in each of the four dimensions.

	Activity		Human Relations		Time		Person-Nature	
	You	Others	You	Others	You	Others	You	Others
1. Job Choice								
15. Ways of Living								
17. Care of Fields								
4. Housework								
20. Nonworking Time								
7. Help in Misfortune								
8. Family Work Relations								
9. Choice of a Delegate								
12. Wage Work								
16. Land Inheritance								
2. Child Training								
5. Expectations about Change								
11. Philosophy of Life								
14. Ceremonial Innovation								
19. Water Allocation								
3. Livestock Dying								
6. Facing Conditions								
10. Maintenance of Gardens								
13. Belief in Control								
18. Length of Life								
	Activity		Human Relations		Time		Person/Nature	
Totals								

KEY FOR ORIENTATIONS	
ACTIVITY A = Doing B = Being	HUMAN RELATIONS A = Lineality (authoritarian) B = Collaterality (consensus) C = Individualism
TIME A = Past B = Present C= Future	PERSON-NATURE A = Subjugation to Nature B = Harmony with Nature C = Mastery over Nature

Activity

Doing: Work hard, apply yourself, and you will be rewarded.
Being: It is enough to just "be"; it's not necessary to accomplish great things to be worthy.

Human Relations

Lineality: Some are born to lead; there are leaders and followers.
Collaterality: Consensus decision making is your preference.
Individualism: The individual should have complete control over his or her own destiny.

Time

Past: Learn from history and emulate the past.
Present: The present moment is everything; enjoy today, don't worry about tomorrow.
Future: Plan and set goals; sacrifice today for a better tomorrow.

Person/Nature

Subjugation to Nature: Humans cannot alter conditions. Life is externally determined by fate, God, genetics.
Harmony with Nature: Humans should strive to live in complete harmony with nature.
Mastery over Nature: Humans' challenge in life is to conquer and control nature.

Adapted from the Kluckhohn "Value Orientations Survey" in *Finding the Middle Ground: Insights and Applications of the Value Orientations Method*, edited by Kurt W. Russo.

51

It's a Puzzle

Time Required

40–60 minutes (20–30 minutes for the game, 20–30 minutes for debriefing)

Objectives

1. To explore the factors that influence the selection or rejection of individuals by a team
2. To provide participants with firsthand experience of being an insider or outsider
3. To explore individual and team behaviors that contribute to meeting an objective
4. To examine how values such as competition and cooperation affect a team when it focuses on "winning"

Materials

- 6 identical puzzles with 12 pieces; (5 sets with 11 pieces each for the teams, placed in envelopes)

  Note: You can create your own puzzles by adhering any picture of your choice to card-stock paper and cutting it into puzzle pieces. Or you can purchase small puzzles in toy stores.

- 3 separate puzzle pieces, only one of which completes the 12-piece puzzle
- 5 envelopes large enough to hold the 11-piece puzzles
- $10 cash in crisp new $1 bills

Process

1. Form participants into equal-sized groups, leaving 3–5 people as "outsiders."
2. Distribute identical puzzle envelopes (with 11 pieces in each) to each team. Announce that the first team to complete its puzzle wins the game.
3. While the teams are busy assembling their puzzles, give a puzzle piece to each of the outsiders. Outsiders can wander around but are not to participate in conversations. Warn the outsiders that they may feel bored and that all but one of them may feel abandoned. Ask them to move about, observing the teams but not becoming involved in the team efforts.

Note: Every team is missing one puzzle piece, the same one. Only one outsider has the piece that is missing from the team puzzles, which means that only one team will have the ability to complete the puzzle.

4. As teams begin to realize that they are missing a piece of their puzzle, announce that each outsider has a puzzle piece and that the outsiders are now permitted to join a team. Outsiders will, however, only visit each team and show their puzzle piece (this is to be done in total silence). After visiting each team, the outsiders will return to the front of the room.

5. Announce a time limit of 3 minutes for the next part of the activity. Ask each team to send a representative to the front of the room to "recruit" any one of the outsiders to join his or her team. Outsiders should listen to recruiters but not announce any decision. Have the recruiters return to their team after the 3 minutes are up.

6. Ask the outsider with the missing puzzle piece to identify the team that he or she would like to join. Stop the outsider from actually joining that team.

7. Now announce that the team that completes the puzzle first will actually win $10. Ask the teams to discuss the implications of this incentive to their recruiting strategy. Give the teams approximately 3 minutes for a discussion, and then announce another recruiting session, also 3 minutes.

8. Ask recruiters to return to teams. Ask the outsider to choose a team. The team completes the puzzle and receives congratulations and the $10.

Debriefing Questions

1. Describe what happened as your team built the puzzle, during the first recruiting session, and during the second recruiting session.
2. How did you feel about how your team assembled the puzzle? In the recruiting session? Do you think your recruiter did a good job?
3. As an outsider, how did you feel during the activity? As the "selected" outsider? As the "rejected" outsider?
4. How did the money incentive influence your recruiting discussion?
5. What values were potentially operating in the behaviors exhibited? What personal values might have contributed to your feelings and behaviors?
6. What have you learned about yourself as a team member? About task/relationship? About outsider/insider behaviors?
7. How might you use the things you learned in your everyday work life?

Debriefing Conclusions

1. Outsiders are often ignored when teams are focused on task.
2. Outsiders receive more attention when they have necessary resources.
3. Being an outsider can generate both positive and negative feelings and behaviors.

4. Introducing rewards into a process can create greater competition or cooperation, based on value systems.

Optional/Additional Debriefing Questions

What happened?

1. What happened at the beginning when you were forming your team (assuming the facilitator had the participants form their own teams)?
2. How did your team go about putting together the puzzle?
3. What happened when the outsiders visited your team?

How do you feel?

1. How do you feel about the way the game was played? Why?
2. Near the end of the game, how did you feel about outsiders who did not have the puzzle piece?
3. Outsiders: How did you feel when the recruiters ignored you? or when all of the teams wanted you?
4. What was your reaction to the winning team's receiving a cash prize?

What did you learn?

1. What did you learn from observing the outsiders without the missing piece? The one with the missing piece?
2. Based on your experience with the game, how do you react to these statements?
   a. You feel happy when people need you.
   b. It is hard not to feel rejected when people ignore you, even if it is not your fault.
   c. When competition is intense and money is involved, people act differently.
   d. Women are more sensitive than men are about rejecting others.
   e. You may want a person for your team, but he or she may not have what it takes to get the job done.

How does this relate?

1. What do the puzzle pieces represent in the real world? *(Note: Watch for competencies, knowledge, and personal characteristics in this discussion).*
2. Who do the outsiders in the game represent? Have you ever felt like an outsider?

What if?

1. What if none of the outsiders had the missing puzzle piece? What if all of the outsiders had the missing piece? The same puzzle piece?
2. What if each team had a different puzzle to construct?
3. What if the winning team received $200?
4. What if the recruiters had more time to persuade the outsider?

Adapted from an activity presented by Sivasailam Thiagarajan at The Summer Institute for Intercultural Communication, 2000.

52

Window to Our World

Adaptable

H

M

Time Required

75 minutes (15 minutes to clarify definitions; 5 minutes for undivided selections; 20 minutes for small-group discussion; 35 minutes for debriefing)

Objectives

1. To examine a group of "isms" and the values reflected by them
2. To explore which "isms" are valued in the participants' culture(s)
3. To explore which "isms" are contradictory to participants' culture(s)
4. To discuss how the differences can impact international business

Materials

- Window to Our World List of "isms" for each participant

Process

1. Give each participant a copy of the "Window to Our World" list of "isms." Explain that an "ism" is a doctrine, theory, or prejudice that supports a particular point of view. Cultures have "isms" that they consider to be right and those they consider to be wrong—all based on the culture's values. *(Note: An option would be to put the dictionary definition of "ism" on a transparency or flipchart and ask the group to develop a definition that fits all of the values in the list.)* Briefly go over the "Window to Our World" list and offer definitions for those "isms" that may be unclear or unknown to anyone. Allow the participants to help describe or explain them briefly. Also allow participants to add additional "isms" that may not be on the list.

2. Ask individuals to identify which "isms" are supported by their culture and which ones are considered wrong. Then ask them to individually select the five they think are most valued and the five they think are least valued in their own culture.

3. Place participants in small groups of 5–7. Instruct them to share the five "isms" they each selected as most and least valued in their culture, as well as why; that is, what cultural values make each "ism" "good" or "bad." Finally, ask participants to discuss the implications of any values differences for conducting international business,

especially if an "ism" is given a positive value in one culture and a negative value in another.

4. Return to the larger group for debriefing.

Debriefing Questions

1. What was easiest to choose, the valued or the least valued "isms"? Hardest? Why?
2. What "isms" were most difficult to discuss in your small group? Why?
3. How did you feel during this activity? Were there differences of opinion in the group discussion that generated strong feelings for you personally?
4. What values do you hold personally that affected your evaluation of these "isms"? Of your group participation? What "isms" were held in common? Which ones were different? Across what cultural groups?
5. What have you learned?
6. How could you apply information from this experience to your work life? Specifically, how would you modify your behaviors if you were working with a culture whose "isms" were contradictory to your own or those of your national or company culture?

Debriefing Conclusions

1. Language (especially "isms") is reflective of cultural values, both positive and negative.
2. The "isms" of one culture may be antagonistic to the cultural values of another culture.
3. Some cultural "isms" will be harder to resolve when conducting business across international borders, while others may make very little difference.
4. Understanding the "isms" (both positive and negative) of the culture with which you are doing business can help you determine whether and/or how to modify your behavior to be most effective in business relationships.

Adapted from an activity in *the Whole World Guide to Culture Learning* by J. Daniel Hess.

Window to Our World List

1. Ageism	19. Industrialism
2. Agnosticism	20. Institutionalism
3. Alcoholism	21. Intellectualism
4. Buddhism	22. Internationalism
5. Capitalism	23. Isolationism
6. Catholicism	24. Judaism
7. Chauvinism	25. Machismo (macho-ism)
8. Collectivism	26. Mysticism
9. Colonialism	27. Parochialism
10. Commercialism	28. Professionalism
11. Communism	29. Progressivism
12. Confucianism	30. Protestantism
13. Conservatism	31. Puritanism
14. Consumerism	32. Racism
15. Feminism	33. Sexism
16. Hedonism	34. Socialism
17. Heterosexism	35. Spiritualism
18. Individualism	

Adapted from an activity in *The Whole World Guide to Culture Learning* by J. Daniel Hess.

A

Appendix

Culture and Values Narrative

I. Definition of Culture

That whole which includes knowledge, beliefs, art, laws, morals, customs, and any capabilities or habits acquired by one as a member of a certain group. Culture is shared by all or almost all members of a group. It is passed on from generation to generation, and it shapes our behavior and structures our perceptions.

II. Components of Culture

Culture has both visible and invisible components. Visible culture includes those things we use our senses for, what we can see, taste, feel, or hear; for example, art, food, music, architecture, clothing, and so forth.

Invisible culture includes those things we do not see either because they are not visible (values) or because we don't think to look for them (communication styles and nonverbal behaviors) or they are outside our consciousness (assumptions).

III. "Invisible" Aspects of Culture

It is the invisible aspects of culture that create the greatest challenges, because we consider our own assumptions, values, behaviors, communication styles, and nonverbal behaviors to be "normal." When someone acts differently from us, we often judge them negatively. Conversely, when they act like us, we either don't pay much attention or we think they are okay. Either conclusion can be incorrect.

IV. Two Types of Values

  A. Terminal values represent the goal we want to achieve.
  B. Instrumental values are the behaviors we use to get to the goal.
  C. We can have similar terminal values and act differently, for example, family may be a value for two people—one person demonstrates that value through the nuclear family; another demonstrates it through the extended family.
  D. We can have different terminal values but act the same; for example, two people work hard to make a lot of money. For one individual, the money is used to support a terminal value of long-

term security for one's family, while another person may be using the money to support a terminal value of material success for oneself.

V. Intent and Impact Are Not the Same!

We might exhibit a behavior with very good intentions, but it may have a negative impact on another person. If we call someone by her or his first name with the intent of being friendly and inclusive, and if that person has a different cultural perspective, our friendly gesture may be experienced as an insult or as disrespect because he or she expects to be addressed formally (Mr., Dr., Ms., Professor).

Similarly, someone may behave in a manner that has a negative impact on us. An Arab might ask, for example, "Why don't you have children?" Our "natural" inclination is to be offended and to want to say, "It's none of your business." The safest assumption, however, is that the person's intention is good. Effective intercultural skills include (a) sharing with others the impact their behavior has had on us and asking them to help us understand their intent, (b) asking about their intent without sharing the impact—which allows us to revise the impact, (c) stating our own intent before acting when behaviors can have multiple interpretations, and/or (d) seeking a wide range of interpretations for the behavior before negatively interpreting it—in other words, avoiding premature judgment.

Activity 27: Seeking Alternative Explanations

Effective cross-cultural behavior includes the ability to seek as many alternative explanations for a person's behavior as possible before evaluating or judging it. In Activity 27, "Visible and Invisible Values" (see page 95), participants will practice first matching behaviors with values and then taking those same behaviors and identifying a range of alternative value explanations for them.

Activity 39: Matching Personal, Team, and Organizational Values

The alignment of personal values with the team and/or organizational values influences performance and job satisfaction. It can also affect customer service, productivity, and profitability. In Activity 39, "Your Values Meet the Team's Values" (see page 157), participants are asked to identify their personal values, then identify team values in small groups in order to determine any barriers to effectiveness based on values differences, and finally to design ways to remove those barriers.

Appendix

Differences in Cultural Values Worksheet

Orientation to Time

Past | Present | Future

Orientation to Activities

Task | Relationship

Formal | Informal

Tradition | Modify | Change

Fixed rules | Flexible rules | No rules

Control actions and outcomes | Control actions but not outcomes | Control neither actions nor outcomes

Orientation to Relationships

Harmony most important | Key issues must be resolved | All issues must be resolved

Individual | One-to-one | Group

Equality | Status earned | Status is given

© Executive Diversity Services, Inc., Seattle, Washington, 1996.

Appendix

Values Differences Handout

Orientation to Time

- *Past* means we look to history to tell us how we should behave in the present. This orientation values history. Today's behaviors should never dishonor, embarrass, or lose face for one's family or ancestors. In deciding what to do today, we might ask "how have we done this in the past?"
- *Present* means the current moment is everything. Make the most of it; don't worry about tomorrow. Planning into the future has limited meaning because, in fact, we cannot know what the future holds. The important question is "What will work for us now?"
- *Future* orientation suggests planning, goal setting, and control over destiny. A little sacrifice today will bring a better tomorrow. The question is "What can we do today that will help us achieve our future goals?"

Orientation to Activities

- *Task* begins with what we need to achieve or do. Relationships are developed as we work together.
- *Relationship* means how we think about, feel about, and work with each other. We develop a relationship, which then helps us accomplish our work together.

- *Formal* approach typically uses status or hierarchy to determine who we work with and how we work together. Titles are used in addressing each other, and hierarchy is strictly followed.
- *Informal* approach assumes equality, resulting in use of first names rather than titles, and allows people to ignore hierarchy to talk and work with anyone who is appropriate to the situation.

- *Tradition* means we do things "the way we have always done them." There is little motivation to change anything that is not seriously ineffective.
- *Modify* refers to the willingness to change how things traditionally have been done if the old way is no longer working very well. This

is not total change but a modification of the old way to fit the new situation or circumstances.

- *Change* means doing something new even if the old way still works. This is an approach of trying something new simply because it might be better or because there is something new to try. Change in itself is the reward.

- *Fixed rules* says that there is an existing rule or law that is applied to everyone in every situation—there are no exceptions.
- *Flexible rules* means that there is a rule, but we appreciate individual situations that can require "exceptions" to the rule. The rule remains for most people or situations, but the rules can be shifted situationally.
- *No rules* says that each situation and each individual are responded to differently. Even if there are written rules, they are rarely used because each person or situation is different.

- *Control actions and outcomes* refers to the belief that the human challenge is to conquer and control nature and events. If we work hard enough and long enough, we can be anything we want to be and do anything we want to do.
- *Control actions but not outcomes* indicates that we can control what we do, but not the outcomes. This is a value often held by those who have worked hard to change their status but have consistently found that external forces have had a greater impact than their own efforts.
- *Control neither actions nor outcomes* is a fatalistic perspective that says life is largely determined by external forces such as God, fate, or genetics; we cannot rise above the conditions life has set.

Orientation to Relationships

- *Harmony most important* means that conflict virtually never occurs. If something you do has a negative impact on me, I will resolve it myself without discussion with you. Conflict or open discussion about discord does not occur.
- *Key issues must be resolved* means that only the bigger issues will be discussed in order to regain harmonious relationships. The smaller issues, those things I can resolve myself, will be managed without discussion.
- *All issues must be resolved* is a value that says I discuss with you virtually everything that is troubling to me so that we can continue to better understand each other and persistently regain or maintain harmonious relationships.

- *Individual* orientation says that we are supposed to take care of ourselves, to be autonomous. We all identify and seek to achieve our own wants and needs, thinking about self first.
- *One-to-One*, or being collateral, means we are both individuals and members of many groups and subgroups. We are both independent and interdependent at the same time. We identify what we want or need in the context of our group membership(s).

- *Group* orientation places the needs of the group first. Individual wants/needs are subordinated to those of the group. In extreme group orientation, the individual may not even be able to identify individual needs/wants outside of the group—the group *is* the individual.

- *Equality* means we are all the same. Regardless of title, age, gender, and so on we all have equal status. An individual can work, communicate, or disagree with any other individual because we are all equal.

- *Status earned* means that some individuals have greater status than others, but we all must earn the respect that comes with the status. A boss, for example, may have the title, but she will receive the respect that comes with the title only by demonstrating that she has earned it.

- *Status given* is an orientation that says if someone has a title, has achieved a certain age, or has a particular role, that person is automatically given respect consistent with the title. Bosses, parents, teachers, and others are never challenged because the title or role itself indicates how they are to be treated, regardless of how they behave.

Sources[*]

Casse, Pierre. *Training for the Cross-Cultural Mind.*

Kluckhohn, Florence, and Fred L. Strodtbeck. *Variations in Value Orientations.*

Lustig, Myron W. "Value Differences in Intercultural Communication." In *Intercultural Communication: A Reader.* 8th ed., edited by Larry A. Samovar and Richard E. Porter.

Stewart, Edward C., and Milton J. Bennett. *American Cultural Patterns: A Cross-Cultural Perspective.* Rev. ed.

[*] See Resource Bibliograpy for complete citations.

Appendix

Cultural Values Lecturette Outline
Does the Difference Make a Difference?

I. Values Continuum
  A. Values fall on a continuum, and our culture teaches us preferences on each continuum.
  B. Our value preferences may fall anywhere on a continuum. Although we can move along the continuum somewhat, we tend to have a preferred place—one where we are most comfortable or to which we turn during times of stress.
  C. We also have learned behaviors that are attached to our preferred value on each continuum.
  D. We can have different values and exhibit the same behavior, or different behaviors to support the same value.
  E. We tend to see a behavior and jump immediately to an interpretation or evaluation of the behavior without first adequately describing that behavior.
  F. If we see different behaviors—or suspect different values—we cannot know what they mean without asking the other person. Using *Describe*, *Interpret*, and *Evaluate* is an effective way to approach behaviors we don't understand or that seem odd. (See Activity 6, "A Value to D.I.E. For," on page 17)

II. What Difference Does the Difference Make?
  A. Once we have asked the other person to interpret the behavior so we know what it means to her or him, we can decide whether that behavior makes a difference.
  B. There are four areas where a behavior *does* make a difference in a workplace:
    1. If the behavior reduces productivity
    2. If the behavior threatens legality—including the laws of the organization, called policies and procedures
    3. If the behavior is unsafe
    4. If the behavior increases costs
  C. If a behavior does none of the above things, then it is *not* a difference that makes a difference, and allowing someone to behave in his or her own manner is an important way to demonstrate that diversity is valued.

D. If the behavior does not make a difference, identify how you might modify your own response to it.

E. If the behavior does make a difference, identify how you are going to tell the individual that the behavior must be modified in this workplace.

Note: Telling someone a behavior does not work in this organization—because it is one of the differences that make a difference—does not mean the behavior is bad or wrong in all contexts. Asking that a behavior stop for one of the above-listed four reasons need not be a negative judgment—only an evaluation about the particular workplace.

Appendix

Stereotypes and Generalizations Lecturette Outline

I. Stereotypes
  A. The word stereotype means "categorizing all members of a group as having the same characteristics."
  B. Stereotypes may or may not be based on tangible facts and can be positive (Asians are good students) or negative (Americans are superficial).
  C. Stereotypes tend to be inflexible and resistant to new information.
  D. They can, and often do, lead to prejudice and intentional or unintentional discrimination (e.g., women are nurturing and will therefore make good nurses).

II. Generalizations
  A. The word generalization means "categorizing many members of a group as having similar characteristics."
  B. Generalizations are based on considerable research or many observations in a wide range of situations.
  C. Generalizations are flexible and open to new information.
  D. They can lead to increased curiosity and awareness and improved cross-cultural relationships (e.g., many women are nurturing, and those who are may be good candidates for the nursing field).

III. Flexibility—the Key Distinction
The most important thing to remember about stereotypes is how inflexible they are. Once we have adopted a stereotype, whether it is conscious or not, our inclination is to believe it is right and to act on it; the stereotype thus becomes entrenched in our responses. Generalizations, on the other hand, allow us a place to begin thinking, but we remain open to examining the situation from other perspectives. This process allows us to revise a generalization based on new information.

IV. The Goal
The goal is to reduce rigidly held stereotypes and encourage more use of generalizations that keep us open to new information and tend to improve relationships.

F

Appendix

Choosing Appropriate Activities for Participants' Developmental Stages

While choosing activities from this manual, keep in mind that individuals learn most effectively if both content and process fit their intellectual and emotional stages of development. This is a particular challenge for classroom settings in which there are individuals in various developmental stages. We do, however, make every effort in our curriculum designs to take groups from less to more challenging content or information and from less to more difficult activities.

One way to express the challenge is to ask participants to learn something (content) or do something (process) that is beyond their current comfort level or ability. It is important to offer enough challenge that the participant is learning but not so much that he or she feels threatened and learning stops. Therefore, we provide more basic information (e.g., the definition of culture) before we provide more complex information (e.g., the definition of values and the distinction between terminal and instrumental values). At the same time we begin with less challenging processes such as "lecturettes" and small-group discussions before moving to more challenging processes such as role playing or simulations.

Janet Bennett (1993) has made the point that it is important to balance the content with the process or activity. She argues that such balance is key to learning. Participants learn most when high-challenge content is balanced with low-challenge process and/or low-challenge content is balanced with high-challenge process:

- High-challenge content and low-challenge process (e.g., understanding values via lecture) = new information
- High-challenge content and high-challenge process (e.g., understanding style shifting via role playing) = threat and escape
- Low-challenge content and low-challenge process (e.g., greeting protocol via lectures) = boredom and escape
- Low-challenge content and high-challenge process (e.g., greeting protocol via physical practice) = new skills

Level of ethnocentrism or ethnorelativism is another developmental perspective that needs to be considered. Milton Bennett (1993) has developed one model for how individuals develop intercultural sensitivity, beginning with the ethnocentric stage of Denial and ending with the ethnorelative stage of Integration. Bennett posits that ethnocentrism, which literally means "centrality of culture," is often the root of cultural misunderstanding and conflict. Individuals learn both the visible/external and invisible/internal rules of their own culture. Thereafter, they tend to assume that the way they see the world is normal and natural and often assume that everyone else views the world the way they do. Ethnorelativism, or relativity of culture, on the other hand, is the ability to see a range of behaviors as appropriate within various cultures. The first step toward cross-cultural competence is cultural self-awareness. Exposure to cultural differences can help provide comparisons to enhance one's self-awareness as well as facilitate the development of multiple frames of reference. Cultural errors can be reduced as an individual's frame of reference expands to include different dimensions of culture.

Bennett's model not only helps identify the stages through which individuals proceed as they approach cultural competency, it also offers suggestions for the most effective types of activities to help people move to the next stage of development.

We have used the work of Milton and Janet Bennett to identify what we believe to be the "risk level" of any given activity for individual participants. Risk is here defined as putting the participants in a situation where they (a) cannot learn new material because it is beyond their developmental stage or intellectual ability, (b) cannot participate in an activity because it is beyond their psychological development or emotional comfort level, or (c) are being asked to disclose something, either behaviorally or verbally, that is embarrassing or seen as too private. Any of these situations may lead to a sense of failure and can result in a participant's withdrawing—either physically or emotionally.

There are also risks for the trainer. A beginning trainer needs to consider her or his depth of information and skill level in facilitating and managing group process. We do not recommend that an inexperienced trainer undertake high-risk activities when working alone. Risk levels for each activity (low, medium, high) are noted in the "Classification of Activities" on pages viii–ix.

Low-risk activities are most appropriate for individuals who may be in the early stages of developing intercultural sensitivity and for whom the very discussion of the content of cultural values may be a relatively risky venture. The activities in *52 Activities for Exploring Values Differences* that allow people to explore culture and values in an easy, nonthreatening manner are presented toward the front of the manual. Higher-risk activities, on the other hand, will be most helpful for people who have had considerable experience with cultural issues and are ready to proceed to more challenging content information or more challenging processes that engage them in personal assessments, self-disclosure, or practice for skill building.

Resource Bibliography

Ackerman, Lawrence D. 2000. *Identity is Destiny: Leadership and the Roots of Value Creation*. San Francisco: Berrett-Koehler Publisher.

Althen, Gary. 2002. *American Ways: A Guide for Foreigners in the United States*. 2d ed. Yarmouth, ME: Intercultural Press.

Barlow, Janelle M. 2000. *Emotional Value: Creating Strong Bonds with Your Customers*. San Francisco: Berrett-Koehler Publisher.

Barrett, Richard. 1998. *Liberating the Corporate Soul: Building a Visionary Organization*. Boston: Butterworth Heinemann.

Bateson, Mary Catherine. 1994. *Peripheral Visions: Learning Along the Way*. New York: Harper Collins Publishers.

Bennett, Janet M. 1993. "Cultural Marginality: Identity Issues in Intercultural Training." In *Education for the Intercultural Experience*, edited by R. Michael Paige. Yarmouth, ME: Intercultural Press.

Bennett, Milton J. 1993. "Toward Ethnorelativism: A Developmental Model of Intercultural Sensitivity." In *Education for the Intercultural Experience*, edited by R. Michael Paige. Yarmouth, ME: Intercultural Press.

———, ed. 1998. *Basic Concepts of Intercultural Communication: Selected Readings*. Yarmouth, ME: Intercultural Press.

Bennett, Milton J., and Janet M. Bennett. 1999. "Description, Interpretation, Evaluation." In "Training for International Transitions," Margaret D. Pusch and Bruce LaBrack. Portland, OR: The Summer Institute for Intercultural Communication.

Casse, Pierre. 1981. *Training for the Cross-Cultural Mind: A Handbook for Cross-Cultural Trainers and Consultants*. Washington, DC: SIETAR.

Cox, Taylor H. 1991. "Effects of Ethnic Group Cultural Differences on Cooperative and Competitive Behavior on Group Task." *Academy of Management Executive* 34, no. 4: 827–47.

Dalton, Maxine A. 1998. "Developing Leaders for Global Roles." In *Center for Creative Leadership Handbook of Leadership Development*, edited by Cynthia D. McCauley, Russ S. Moxley, and Ellen Van Velsor, 379–402. San Francisco: Jossey-Bass.

Deal, Terrence E. 1986. *Corporate Cultures: The Rites and Rituals of Corporate Life*. Reading, MA: Addison-Wesley.

Fowler, Sandra M., and Monica G. Mumford, eds. 1999. *Intercultural Sourcebook: Cross-Cultural Training Methods*, vol. 2. Yarmouth, ME: Intercultural Press.

———, eds. 1995. *Intercultural Sourcebook: Cross-Cultural Training Methods*, vol. 1. Yarmouth, ME: Intercultural Press.

Gardenswartz, Lee, and Anita Rowe. 1994. *Diverse Teams at Work: Capitalizing on the Power of Diversity*. New York: McGraw-Hill.

Gudykunst, William B. 1991. *Bridging Differences: Intergroup Interaction*. Newbury Park, CA: Sage.

Hall, Brian P. 1998. *Personal Workbook: Understanding and Working with Values*. Napa, CA: Values Technology.

———. 1995. *Values Shift: A Guide to Personal and Organizational Transformation*. Rockport, MA: Twin Lights.

Hall, Brian P., and Martin L. W. Hall. 1999. *Understanding and Working with Values*. Napa, CA: Values Technology.

———. 1998. *Building Cultures of Excellence: Getting Started with Values*. Napa, CA: Values Technology.

Hall, Brian P., O. Harari, B. D. Ledig, and M. Tondor. 1986. *Manual for the Hall-Tonna Inventory of Values*. Mahwah, NJ: Paulist Press.

Hall, Edward T. 1983. *The Dance of Life: The Other Dimension of Time*. New York: Anchor/Doubleday.

———. 1959 [1981]. *The Silent Language*. New York: Anchor/Doubleday.

Hammer, Mitchell R. 1998. "A Measure of Intercultural Sensitivity: The Intercultural Developmental Inventory." In *Intercultural Sourcebook: Cross-Cultural Training Methods*, vol. 2, edited by Sandra M. Fowler and Monica G. Mumford, 1–13. Yarmouth, ME: Intercultural Press.

Hampden-Turner, Charles. 1990. *Charting the Corporate Mind: Graphic Solutions to Business Conflict*. New York: Macmillan.

Hampden-Turner, Charles, and Fons Trompenaars. 1993. *The Seven Cultures of Capitalism: Value Systems for Creating Wealth*. New York: Doubleday.

Hess, J. Daniel. 1997. *Studying Abroad/Learning Abroad*. Yarmouth, ME: Intercultural Press.

———. 1994. *The Whole World Guide to Culture Learning*. Yarmouth, ME: Intercultural Press.

Hofstede, Geert. 1997. *Culture and Organizations, Software of the Mind: Intercultural Cooperation and Its Importance for Survival*. New York: McGraw-Hill.

———. 1985. "The Interaction between National and Organizational Value Systems." *Journal of Management Studies* 22, no. 4: 347–57.

———. 1980. *Culture's Consequences: International Differences in Work Related Values*. Beverly Hills: Sage.

Jackofsky, Ellen S., and Sara J. Mcquaid. 1988. "Cultural Values and the CEO: Alluring Companions." *Academy of Management Executive* 2, no. 1: 39–49.

Kluckhohn, Florence R. 2000. "Value Orientations Survey." In *Finding the Middle Ground: Insights and Applications of the Value Orientations Method*, edited by Kurt W. Russo. Yarmouth, ME: Intercultural Press.

———. 1961. *Variations in Value Orientations*. Evanston, IL: Row, Peterson.

Kohls, L. Robert, and Herbert L. Brussow. 1995. *Training Know-How for Cross-Cultural and Diversity Trainers*. Ducanville, TX: Adult Learning Systems.

Kohls, L. Robert, and John M. Knight. 1994. *Developing Intercultural Awareness: A Cross-Cultural Training Handbook*. 2d ed. Yarmouth, ME: Intercultural Press.

Kolb, David A. 1985. *LSI Learning Style Inventory: Self-Scoring Inventory and Interpretation Booklet*. Boston: McBer and Company.

Kolb, David A., and D. M. Smith. 1985. *User's Guide for the Learning Style Inventory*. Boston: McBer and Company.

Landis, Dan, and Rabi S. Bhagat. 1996. *Handbook of Intercultural Training*. 2d ed. Thousand Oaks, CA: Sage.

Laurent, Andre. 1999. "Reinventing Management at the Cross-Roads of Culture." Portland, OR: The Summer Institute for Intercultural Communication.

Leslie, Jean B., and Ellen Van Velsor. 1998. *A Cross-National Comparison of Effective Leadership and Teamwork: Toward a Global Workforce*. Greensboro, NC: Center for Creative Leadership.

Lustig, Myron W. 1997. "Value Differences in Intercultural Communication." In *Intercultural Communication: A Reader*. 8th ed., edited by Larry A. Samovar and Richard E. Porter. Belmont, CA: Wadsworth.

Paige, R. Michael, ed. 1993. *Education for the Intercultural Experience*. 2d ed. Yarmouth, ME: Intercultural Press.

Pusch, Margaret D., ed. 1979. *Multicultural Education: A Cross-Cultural Training Approach*. Yarmouth, ME: Intercultural Press.

Pusch, Margaret D., and Bruce LaBrack. 1999. "Training for International Transitions." Portland, OR: The Summer Institute for Intercultural Communication.

Pusch, Margaret D., and Jaime Wurzel. 1999. "Foundations of Intercultural Communication." Portland, OR: The Summer Institute for Intercultural Communication.

Rokeach, Milton. 1973. *The Nature of Human Values*. New York: The Free Press.

Rowe, Anita, 1993. "Understanding Diversity Blind Spots in the Performance Review." *CUPA Journal* (winter).

Russo, Kurt W., ed. 2000. *Finding the Middle Ground: Insights and Applications of the Value Orientations Method*. Yarmouth, ME: Intercultural Press.

Samovar, Larry A., and Richard E. Porter, eds. 1997. *Intercultural Communication: A Reader*. 8th ed. Belmont, CA: Wadsworth.

Schein, Edgar H. 1999. *Corporate Culture: Survival Guide*. San Francisco: Jossey-Bass.

————. 1992. *Organizational Culture and Leadership*. 2d ed. San Francisco: Jossey-Bass.

————. 1989. "Corporate Culture Is the Real Key to Creativity." *Business Month* 5, 73–74.

Seelye, H. Ned, ed. 1996. *Experiential Activities for Intercultural Learning*. Yarmouth, ME: Intercultural Press.

Seelye, H. Ned, and Alan Seelye-James. 1996. *Culture Clash: Managing in a Multicultural World*. Lincolnwood, IL: NTC.

Senge, Peter M. 1999. *The Dance of Change*. New York: Doubleday.

————. 1990. *The Fifth Discipline: The Art and Practice of the Learning Organization*. New York: Doubleday.

Senge, Peter M., Art Kleiner, C. Roberts, R. Ross, and B. Smith. 1994. *The Fifth Discipline Fieldbook: Strategies and Tools for Building a Learning Organization*. New York: Doubleday.

Stewart, Edward C., and Milton J. Bennett. 1991. *American Cultural Patterns: A Cross-Cultural Perspective*. Rev. ed. Yarmouth, ME: Intercultural Press.

Storti, Craig. 2001. *The Art of Coming Home*. Yarmouth, ME: Intercultural Press.

————. 2001. *The Art of Crossing Cultures*. 2d ed. Yarmouth, ME: Intercultural Press.

————. 1999. *Figuring Foreigners Out: A Practical Guide*. Yarmouth, ME: Intercultural Press.

————. 1994. *Cross-Cultural Dialogues: 74 Brief Encounters with Cultural Difference*. Yarmouth, ME: Intercultural Press.

Stringer, Donna M., and Steve Guy. 1998. "Using Values-Based Performance Feedback to Motivate Employees." *Employment Relations Today*, Winter, 73–82.

Summerfield, Ellen. 1993. *Crossing Cultures through Film*. Yarmouth, ME: Intercultural Press.

Thiagarajan, Sivasailam. 2000. "Interactive Experiential Strategies for Multicultural Learning." Portland, OR: The Summer Institute for Intercultural Communication.

Triandis, Harry C. 1994. *Culture and Social Behavior*. New York: McGraw-Hill.

Trompenaars, Fons, and Charles Hampden-Turner. 1998. *Riding the Waves of Culture: Understanding Diversity in Global Business*. New York: McGraw-Hill.

Zemke, Ron, Claire Raines, and Bob Filipczak. 2000. *Generations at Work: Managing the Clash of Veterans, Boomers, Xers and Nexters in Your Workplace*. New York: AMACOM.

About the Authors

Donna M. Stringer, Ph.D., is president of Executive Diversity Services Inc., a Seattle-based management consulting and employee training firm. Her doctoral degree in social/developmental psychology has led to a thirty-year career working as a teacher, senior trainer, instructional designer, researcher and writer in addition to her current position. As a consultant, she applies theory and practice to work team interventions, trainer education, and executive coaching. Since 1994, Stringer has been a faculty member of The Summer Institute for Intercultural Communication. She is also adjunct faculty at Seattle University, University of Washington, and Antioch University, where she teaches a variety of international business, management and intercultural courses.

Patricia A. Cassiday, Ed.D., is an adjunct professor at Seattle University and a professional coach, specializing in the support of cross-cultural transition for individuals and families. While working as a counselor in Germany, Cassiday served as a consultant on topics related to international transition, third culture kids, comprehensive guidance, and conflict resolution. As a certified counselor, educator, curriculum developer and expatriate, Cassiday brings her special combination of skills to this book.

Donna Stringer is available as a trainer or consultant in the subjects covered in this book. She can be reached at
e-mail: dstringer@executivediversity.com
phone: 206-224-9293
fax: 206-224-9303

Patricia Cassiday is available as a coach or consultant in the subjects covered in this book. She can be reached at
e-mail: cassiday@collaborativeconnection.com
phone: 425-373-0139
fax: 425-373-0139